Direct
10.⁰⁰
28Jul'78

THE
JAMES SPRUNT STUDIES
IN HISTORY
AND POLITICAL SCIENCE

*Published under the Direction of
the Departments of History and Political Science
of The University of North Carolina at Chapel Hill*

VOLUME 56

Editors

J. CARLYLE SITTERSON, *Chairman*
FEDERICO G. GIL
JOHN D. MARTZ
GEORGE D. TAYLOR
GEORGE B. TINDALL

CHANGE
AND
BUREAUCRACY

PUBLIC ADMINISTRATION
IN VENEZUELA

by
Bill Stewart

CHAPEL HILL
THE UNIVERSITY OF NORTH CAROLINA PRESS
1978

Copyright © 1978 by
The University of North Carolina Press
All rights reserved
Manufactured in the United States of America
ISBN 0-8078-5056-X
Library of Congress Catalog Card Number 77-18192

Library of Congress Cataloging in Publication Data

Stewart, William Stanley, 1938–
   Public Administration

   (The James Sprunt studies in history and political
science; v. 56)
   Bibliography: p.
   Includes index.
   1. Venezuela—Politics and government—1935–
2. Bureaucracy. 3. Venezuela—Officials and employees
—Attitudes. I. Title. II. Series.
JL3831.S75   354'.87   77-18192
ISBN 0-8078-5056-X

TABLE OF CONTENTS

TABLES

PREFACE

This book is about public administration in Venezuela. My interest in Venezuela dates from 1962, when I began teaching English in the University of the East in Ciudad Bolívar. During the next two years I taught on three different campuses of the university, spending most of my time at the School of Basic Studies in Cumaná. I came away with a much better understanding of the problems individuals face in Venezuela when they attempt to function as professionals within normal bureaucratic structures there. Many of these problems seemed abnormal and unnecessary at first, their only possible cause being the personalities of the people involved. With time it became apparent that the systems within which individuals function in Venezuela severely restrict the range of options and strategies available to them. Since leaving the university in 1964 I have spent some time in trying to understand what was happening in Venezuela while I was there. The options and strategies the system allow have become clearer to me, and this work is an effort to examine the relation between bureaucratic culture and the attitudes of individual bureaucrats in Venezuela.

The first part of this book deals with the nature of public administration in Venezuela, the historical factors that created it, and its place in national life. History and culture have been discussed at some length, for the aim of this section is to provide the reader with the context within which the following work must be seen. The second part reports the results of an attitude survey of 153 Venezuelan public administrators. My aim was to find out what these people thought about themes that had emerged again and again in the interminable discussions in eastern Venezuela ten years earlier: efficiency, innovation and personal responsibilities—efficiency in doing our jobs, innovation in changing the authority patterns and values that seemed to us to be keeping us from doing our jobs, and the responsibilities to our families and to ourselves that many felt limited our options. The survey also asked the respondents their opinions on some strategies of reform available to the government.

In the last part of the book I attempt to put together what I have learned about Venezuelan public administration and the likelihood and desirability of reforming it. Discussions of theories of reform and bureaucracy have been included at different points throughout the work where they would seem to be most appropriate. Change in society and individual lives is the most important concept used and, I hope, the one most illuminated by our research. At a time in American history when we are finally approaching the limits of our physical resources, the study of change would seem especially appropriate. I hope the following work will help us understand our own problems in dealing with change as well as it does those in Venezuela.

This study is the result of research done in Venezuela with the cooperation of the Venezuelan Commission on Public Administration and the Northern Inter-American Center for Training in Public Administration of the Organization of American States. Sponsored by the Public Administration Unit of the OAS, the primary object of the study was to aid the Commission in its goal of administrative reform. While this report contains some tentative recommendations to the Commission and its School of Public Administration, it is best seen as basic research into some of the values and attitudes held by a rather select group of Venezuela's public administrators. The graduate students of the National School of Public Administration, the Commission's teaching branch, have a particular importance to the Commission's hopes for administrative reform, for they are the people who, returning to their different organizations, will be looked to as the apostles of the Commission's reform efforts. It is hoped that this study will be of use to the Commission in understanding these men and women, and that their views on some of the strategies of reform the Commission is considering will also be useful.

Special thanks are owed Dr. Allan-Randolph Brewer-Carias, the President of the Commission, and Dr. Moisés Lichtmajer, the Director of the Inter-American Center in Caracas. Both were instrumental in the success of the survey and were always ready to help when help was needed. Their interest and advice were extremely valuable in the earlier stages of the survey and their continued support has been greatly appreciated. Special thanks are also due Dr. Ligia Valladares de Salcedo, Director of the Commission's research department. Her friendship and professional knowledge constantly supported the research, contributing to the study in all its phases. The defects of the work are, of course, attributable to its author. It is hoped that they are outweighed by whatever merit it may have and that it will prove to be of use to the Commission.

Dr. Alberto Torrentes Vieira, Director of the Public Administration Unit of the OAS, has supported the work from its inception and has been a major factor in its completion. His kindness and continuing support have been greatly appreciated. A great debt is also owed Rogerio Pinto, the primary advisor from the Public Administration Unit for the paper. His friendship and readiness to help have made inconsequential many problems which without him could easily have been major obstacles.

A major debt is owed my friend and advisor at the University of North Carolina, Professor Robert T. Daland. Both the research methods and the major theoretical concerns of this work are derived from his studies of development administration. Without his counsel, critcism, and support this study would not have taken place.

One other person has had a major input to this study. Without the time and energy contributed by my wife, Elizabeth C. Stewart, I would not have been able to collect the data upon which it is based. Her excellent knowledge of Spanish and deep understanding of the Venezuelan people and their culture were extremely valuable in contacting and interviewing the respondents. Working as a team we were able to do far more than I could have achieved working alone.

I should also like to give my special thanks to Federico Gil and John Martz, who have offered unfailing support and encouragement throughout my academic career and, in Federico's case, since my Peace Corps training in 1962. I owe them both a great deal, and would like to acknowledge them here.

PART I

BUREAUCRATIC CONTEXT

I.

AUTHORITY AND CONTROL

Venezuela is located on the southern shore of the Caribbean Sea. It is a relatively large country, about the size of Texas and Oklahoma combined, but the great majority of its inhabitants live either in the Venezuelan Andes or the Coastal Highlands, regions which together constitute about one third of the nation. The rest of the country is very hot, very uncomfortable and was, until DDT and technologically advanced public health services reached it in the 1940s, very sick. With limited agricultural resources, few Indians, and no gold, Venezuela was considered a backwater by most other Latin Americans for centuries.

With the discovery of oil in 1913 Venezuela became important to the United States and the great international oil companies, but there was little immediate change inside the country. The oil revenues enabled the fortunate dictator of the moment to extend his reign to a quarter of a century and to more or less own the country at the time of his death, but little occurred to change the daily lives of most Venezuelans. Technologically advanced systems of communication and transportation were introduced, but they were mainly used to aggressively maintain traditional patterns of government and traditional culture. Mass-based political parties began organizing ordinary Venezuelans in the late 1930s, but it was not until 1958 and the political triumph of the democratic parties that national changes in culture and government came into the open.

Since 1958 Venezuela has been governed by democratic regimes dedicated to the development of the country, both in terms of industrial and agricultural production and in terms of the social and economic welfare of the Venezuelan people. These goals require massive governmental funding, primarily because the basic wealth of the nation has not been generated within the country but is rather a product of taxation and profit sharing with oil companies. The result is a very large amount of money that must be controlled by the government apparatus. Moreover, Venezuelan governments have traditionally accepted the idea that the national government is responsible for both planning and initiating national growth, and in many recent cases have also felt that national agencies should be responsible for the production of that wealth. Since 1958 they have also generally agreed that the government should be responsible for the welfare of the people, a commitment requiring large bureaucracies if it is to be effectively implemented. The nature and functioning of the public administration is consequently of great importance to Venezuelans, and it is not surprising that the democratic governments have made major efforts to increase its effectiveness. Before dealing with these efforts at reform, however, we shall review the nature of the bureaucracy, its present environment, and the strategies different agencies have developed to cope with the changes that have come in the last thirty years.

The general observation that public administration in Venezuela is centralized, authoritarian, and very open to political influence is a realistic view, although it is important to remember that within this general framework there is a great deal of latitude for both individual and institutional variety. A tradition and desire for autonomy especially allow for the development of distinctive organizations and are often of positive value to those bureaucrats especially interested in the achievement of their agency's overt goals. Even then, however, the attributes noted above continue to operate. Probably the most serious of these problems for the traditional student of public administration would be that of political influence.

The type of political influence referred to is the straightforward use of party membership and influence to affect the implementation of national law. Such influence is usually routed through local party leaders to the national party heads and from them to the presidency or to the minister involved, and from that office to the local branch of the agency. That is, people wishing to influence agency behavior do not have effective direct lines to the local agency but are forced to operate through the political system in order to reach the locus of agency authority.[1] This implies, of course, that local corruption is not a great problem and that the bureaucratic system is effectively centralized.

The amount and kind of political influence of this type that an agency has to deal with is directly related to two differing factors: (1) the degree of direct involvement in the agency's work with people and (2) the degree of consensus within the nation on the policy the agency is implementing. The Ministry of Mines and Hydrocarbons, for example, deals almost entirely with foreign companies and implements a policy that represents the overwhelming consensus of all the political parties. Mines and Hydrocarbons has a well-deserved reputation for both effectiveness and efficiency. While it is a crucial agency, and therefore liable to closer scrutiny and more continuous supervision than others, it has been free of the sort of political influence described above. Since the nationalization of the oil industry in January 1976 the Ministry of Mines and Hydrocarbons has become responsible for the production of oil and is presumably more exposed to influence than before. On the other hand, the relatively small number of workers employed, the tremendous importance of the industry to the nation, and the appointment of the highly regarded head of the Venezuelan Guayana Corporation as head of the public corporation responsible for production all indicate that political influence in this ministry will remain small in comparison with other less technically oriented agencies.[2]

The Ministry of Education has as its reason for existence the direct influencing of great numbers of people in ways that are clearly of great importance to them. Moreover, there is a significant lack of consensus in Venezuela on just what education is supposed to do for people. Before 1958 the general view of education was that it was an attribute of social and economic status. Since 1958 all political parties have agreed that there should be a lot more of it, but exactly what an education is for has been a matter of dispute. Most national leaders have agreed that the goals of education should generally be those of equipping people with skills needed by the technological economy they are attempting to build. A deeper understanding of education, and one strongly held by a large number of people, is the older idea of education as an attribute of class. Moreover, this conviction is frequently reversed by students and their families to a belief that a degree is an assurance of status. When teachers also share this belief, as many of them do, the negative consequences for technical proficiency are enormous.[3]

A contributing factor to the troubles of the Ministry of Education is that the decision was made in 1958 to more than double the student population and to make the only requirement for entrance into higher levels of education a successful exit from the lower ones. It was easier and quicker to build schools than to train teachers, and the result was a massively underqualified teaching corps in the 1960s. Although the ministry has systematically upgraded these teachers through in-service training and night courses, the consequences for students and the system itself were and are enormous. Unqualified teachers produce unqualifed students, but these students have legitimate aspirations, and, given the circumstances, can hardly be blamed for their scholastic inadequacy. On the other hand, the educational bureaucracy can scarcely be said to be doing its job if large numbers of technically unqualified students are graduated. The problem is complicated by the deep ambiguity with which many Venezuelans view a technologically oriented career. There is a strong tendency to see the question as Humanism versus Technology in a culture in which the former is clearly the side of the angels. That the educational bureaucracy is as involved in this cultural transition as the students who are its responsibility is not surprising, particularly in view of the rapid expansion of the teaching corps. The point is that the Ministry of Education is intimately involved in what might be termed a "people" problem, whereas the Ministry of Mines and Hydrocarbons is not. It is obvious that the Ministry of Education will be the object of intense and continuous pressure and, given the nature and use of Venezuelan political parties, that this pressure will be channeled through the political parties. The lack of consensus on what an education is for and the simultaneous consensus that as many people as possible must be educated result in a high degree of what we have termed "political influence" on Education. A low degree of political influence is exerted on Mines and Hydrocarbons because it is not involved in these areas. This is not to say that consensus as such is either necessary or healthy, but to point out the consequences it has for bureaucratic organizations in Venezuela. Political influence on the bureaucracy in democratic Venezuela is not constant for all agencies, but varies directly with the degree to which the agency is involved with "people" problems rather than those that can be more narrowly defined as "technical" issues. To anticipate a bit, one strategy for an agency desiring to gain freedom from political pressures would be to define its work wherever possible as "technical" rather than "people" oriented. The Ministry of Education does not have a very good chance of carrying this off successfully.

Centralization is much more uniform throughout the bureaucracy than political pressure. All national agencies have their headquarters in Caracas, and decisions, of any consequence at all are normally made there. In fact, all decisions, whether important or not, are usually made in Caracas. Mitigating factors are the effective size of the country in demographic terms and the generally good communications system.

The physical and cultural disparities between Caracas and the rest of the country are great, however, and have a negative effect upon national administration. Given the cosmopolitan and technologically sophisticated nature of life in the capital it is not unusual for administrators to lose their perspective on the interior and come to view it as a rather alien and backward area, qualitatively different from their own world and, consequently, from them. Cultural assumptions of this sort tend to hinder communications and generally assume that enlightenment resides only at the center.

State governments might be expected to counteract this attitude, but in the Venezuelan case they tend to reinforce it. Although state legislatures are elected bodies, they have little control over either the governor or state finances. Both governorships and money are allocated by the national center, the former being appointed by the president and the latter being disbursed almost entirely through national agencies. The governor's role, in fact, is to represent the national government, to coordinate national programs, and to maintain order and tranquility. His power is that of a high party man, and it is exercised through the party. When the national government is made up of a coalition of parties, as it usually has been since 1958, a governor may operate more as a representative of his party than of the president if his party does not control the presidency.[4] The effect upon bureaucrats in this case is to give them a little more leeway, but the national focus remains and the routes of influence are the same.

Local governments have historically been the holders of residual powers. Given the pervasive nature of the formal Spanish state, these were minimal. They have been exercised most when the central government has broken down. Since 1962 there has been a government-sponsored effort to establish local governments as major political and bureaucratic forces within Venezuela, but the issue remains in doubt.

The national government has also made an effort to regionalize the bureaucracy by requiring it to set up regional offices in eight areas specified by law. This is a relatively recent development (1969) and it is debatable whether many agencies have in fact delegated authority to these offices. The general opinion is that they have not done so and that the major accomplishment of the law has been to require a new set of initials on communications routed to the agency head.

Effective state and local governments and the delegation of authority to regional centers would all run counter to the well-established pattern of authoritarianism that exists in most Venezuelan agencies. The centralization noted above is partly physical, in that virtually all governmental agencies are run from Caracas, but it is basically a centralization of authority. The traditional situation is that leadership is a prerogative exercised only by the head of the agency and that all effective lines of communication to and from this leader are personal. Preoccupation with personal ties and loyalties is high, and other considerations are often slighted because of this. The connection between an authoritarian style of leadership and "personalism" is strong, as we have lately seen in the United States. In Venezuela the classic case has been that of the "strong man" (the caudillo), and the usual leader/follower relationship has been that of patron to client. The immediate circle around the leader is termed the *rosca*, a generic term meaning about the same as "mafia" has lately come to mean in the United States. The "Irish Mafia" of President Kennedy and the "German Mafia" of President Nixon are good examples. A less pejorative term might be "management team." At any rate, bureaucratic leaders in Venezuela do generally have roscas, and the ties within these roscas are very personal.

The main problem with authoritarian leadership patterns in the bureaucracy is that binding decisions are reserved to the leader and that formal communications are decidedly secondary in effectiveness to those reaching the leader through his personal contacts. The effect is that an agency is paralyzed for any but the most routine actions when its leadership is elsewhere. That is, given that the agency is fairly large and complex, any meaningful decision must become a crisis before it can compete for the leader's attention. Once the leader's time and attention have been captured, the crisis (if it is not too complex) can often be solved in short order, since the leader has both the authority and the staff to deal with it. Given a minimum number of crises and a capable leader, this style of leadership can be very effective.[5]

One of the main requirements for a small number of crises, however, is a stable culture and a national policy of maintaining that culture. Venezuela's economy and culture are both changing daily, and the advantages of authoritarian bureaucratic leadership are outweighed by its disadvantages. The time and effort that must be expended in gaining the leaders' attention are so large that most bureaucratic executives outside Caracas find it expedient to send a messenger with routine requests and to travel to Caracas whenever an important decision is needed. Within Caracas the same system is followed, although here the advantages of a messenger over the mail service are obvious and less time is lost in traveling. The drain upon subordinates' time and energy is great and its effect upon efficiency can only be negative.

The leader's time is also finite. Higher executives in Venezuela are typically conscientious and hardworking, but they are also typically behind in meeting the crises that are continually piling up before them. Add to this the time taken in dealing with the political pressures inevitably brought to bear on the head of an agency, and the picture is complete.

Control of Implementation

A serious consequence of all this is that it is very difficult for agency heads to maintain control over the implementation of their policies. The reason is that the more authority is centralized in the head of the agency, the more difficult it is for those actually implementing the agency's policy to get necessary decisions on time. If economics and culture in Venezuela were unchanging, few decisions would be necessary since the regulations of the agency would fully cover the problems encountered. In reality neither of these factors is stable and regulations are often not well suited for the situations in which the agency's operating personnel find themselves. Decisions on changing regulations take even longer than decisions on individual cases, and consequently emphasis tends to be put upon individual solutions to individual cases. Since all of these must compete for the leader's attention, the temptation is great for line personnel to short-circuit the whole process by informally solving the problem through the falsification of forms and reports. It is important to note that "corruption," in the sense of payment for services rendered and risks taken, need not be a primary motive or even present. The problems lie in the difficulties of getting authoritative decisions and in applying static regulations to fluid situations.

As Riggs has noted,[6] a logical response to this situation is to increase the supervision of subordinates and to curtail even further the area of their authority. This, however, sets off a vicious circle as well as presenting the inspectors themselves with increased opportunities for "corruption." Carried to its logical extreme such "corruption" is necessary if the system is to work at all, but it has the regrettable effect of vitiating adherence to formal rules while at the same time providing strong motives for the increased production of these same formal regulations in order to increase the occasions for payoffs.

The Venezuelan situation has not proceeded this far and shows no persuasive signs of doing so. While corruption was widespread under Marcos Pérez Jiménez (dictator, 1950–58), it has not been a serious problem under the democratic regimes that have followed him. Partly this is a consequence of the wealth of the country: Venezuela has been able to afford relatively good salaries for governmental personnel. A stronger factor may be that of the present political organization of the country. With a highly organized citizenry the parties have been able to use their influence to hold the bureaucracy accountable. Before exploring this possibility further we will examine the cultural and structural background of the Venezuelan bureaucracy.

II.

BUREAUCRATIC HISTORY

Perhaps the most important factor in the Spanish administration of the American colonies was the legal and moral assumption that they were the personal property of the king.[1] This, coupled with the fact that all laws were written in Spain by the Council of the Indies, set the stage for administration that was intensely personal at the same time it was intensely legalistic. In theory, all behavior was to be judged by and adjusted to the laws drawn up by the council; local administrators had no power to make or adjust these laws. Two other elements of Spanish thought must be understood before dismissing the system as a completely unworkable monstrosity. First, the codes set up by the council were intended to serve much the same purpose as Latin American constitutions are intended to serve in the present: they embody the ideals of the nation. They are meant to be and are thought of as expressive of what the nation ought to be, and as such are clear statements of the best aspirations of men. They are also, however, working documents meant to guide the ordinary actions of government. Most Latin American constitutions provide for circumstances in which the real situation is too out of step with the ideal by including a provision for the suspension of the constitution itself. That is, when men so forget their ideals as to render government by those ideals impossible the president and Congress are allowed to suspend them until the situation has been corrected.

Such a system is obviously open to great abuse, and this was as clearly recognized in colonial times as it is today. The personalistic aspect of the king's relations to his subjects was the element that allowed a formally rigid system to overcome its consequent unreality. The first great challenge to the system occurred early in the colonial age.[2] The enslavement and savage treatment of the native inhabitants of America by the Spanish was condoned neither by the king nor by the church. When the abuses became known, the first reaction was to pass laws specifically forbidding such acts. In response to what was felt by the colonists to be a clearly unrealistic law, the doctrine of "obedezco pero no cumplo" was enunciated.

"I obey but do not comply" was a direct appeal to the personal relation the king was felt to have with each of his subjects. In the case under discussion it roughly meant that the individual colonist who had enslaved Indians freely accepted the principle that the king had every right to order him not to enslave the Indians, but that the king did not understand that such a development would be ruinous to the king himself. Therefore the colonist, who did understand this, would not comply with the order in order to protect his king. Moreover, he would personally come to the king to explain the situation to him. That is, he would disregard the whole administrative structure the king had developed by going directly to the king. The king was in fact eventually convinced of (1) the difficulties in exploiting the New World without the enforced labor of the Indians and (2) the manifest impossibility of preventing the colonists from using that labor. The solution was to work out a system of vassalage in which the Indians were neither free nor slaves. They were recognized as subjects of the crown with certain definable rights and privileges but had the duty of serving those individuals appointed by the king as their lords. Before condemning this system North Americans should remember what happened to Blacks in the United States, a country with a highly "realistic" constitution and legal system.

The basic elements of legalism and personalism were thus set very early on in Venezuela, but several corollary systems were also relevant to contemporary administration. The system that the king had set up was obviously open to abuses, all of which would not be overcome through individuals appealing directly to the king. In order to overcome the possibility that official communications would only present the king and his council with information which the bureaucracy wanted him to have, several official bodies were created with overlapping responsibilities and prerogatives. Basically, these were the executive hierarchy (viceroys, captains general, presidents, etc.), the judicial hierarchy (the *audiencia*), and the inspectors (*auditores*). Citizens of substance could appeal to any or all of these with a very good chance of preventing or at least delaying the action of another branch. Moreover, the church could also function within this system as a separate actor, thus giving the poor and oppressed an avenue for redress of wrongs.

For some three hundred years this system worked very well. The king maintained legal control over the New World, he received on a regular basis a great amount of wealth, and he did both of these without a standing army in the colonies. Moreover, after the first fifty years the system did prevent some of the worst abuses of men against men and provided a very fair amount of stability and social order.

The cost was the imposition of a static social system and a widespread view that the law in its details was both unrealistic and largely unenforceable. Trade and industry became in large part smuggling and illicit manufacture. While many of the colonies did develop and change, it was more in opposition to the law than because of it, a situation that could hardly result in any but the most perfunctory recognition of law as applicable to actual human behavior.

One other aspect of colonial administration should be noted here. The possibility that the competing authorities in the colonies would combine against the king's interests was obvious, and it could only be encouraged if key governmental positions were filled by the colonists. The solution was to fill these positions only with Spaniards who would return to Spain and therefore would retain their loyalty to the king. In the event, this system was extended to virtually all administrative positions in the colonies, and its relation to the rosca prevalent in the contemporary Venezuelan administrative system is clear.

The politics of the republic created in 1830 revolved around who would control the government rather than how it would function. During the nineteenth century the continuing struggle among regional caudillos for control of the national government did not basically change the culture, society, or economic structure of the country. Indeed, until Gómez (Juan Vicente Gómez, dictator, 1908–35) the political structure changed very little either, in that it continued to revolve around regional forces that essentially fulfilled the function of the differing organs of government of the king. The theoretical basis of government had changed with the promulgation of the new constitution, but due to the cultural understanding of the functions of law and legal institutions described above it had little impact upon the lives of most people. From 1830 to 1930 life and culture in Venezuela changed very little.

Governmental structure, on the other hand, had experienced more or less continual growth and differentiation during this period. The government of 1830 had established three secretariats responsible (respectively) for justice and government, finance and foreign affairs, and defense.[3] By 1930 these secretariats had grown to eight ministries (Interior and Justice, Health and Agriculture, Development, Education, Public Works, Treasury, Foreign Affairs, and Defense) and the Office of the President. Their general pattern of development is one of organizational stability once ministerial status has been secured. There has been some shifting of departments among ministries, but the usual process is that a department develops within a single ministry (generally Development) until it emerges as an independent body. While Venezuelan presidential politics may have been chaotic during the state's first century of independent existence, the machinery of government remained stable.

This is consistent with the idea that unstable presidential politics have as their natural consequence a bureaucracy largely independent of presidential control. Primarily advanced by Riggs,[4] this argument holds that since the various agencies of the public administration are the only government organizations that are continuous, their personnel, especially at the middle levels, are able to entrench themselves in their positions and to provide the minimum stability in governmental services that all societies need in order to continue in existence as viable states. Unstable presidential politics, which might seem to be a danger to administrative stability, actually tend to reinforce it. This is so because (1) if the presidential group is interested in enrichment, then the bureaucracy can more or less purchase its continued existence through the provision of jobs, sinecures, and "gifts"; and (2) if the presidency is interested in reform and effective government, it needs the bureaucracy in order to carry out its programs.

To find either of these situations in a pure form would be highly unusual. Few governments are committed to graft and nothing else, and equally few find themselves in a position where some degree of patronage and the use of government to pay political debts is unnecessary. Both factors tend to reinforce the functional independence of the bureaucracy, for both require a continuing stable organization in order to function.

The bureaucracy is also a political actor itself, having as its minimal input most if not all of the information upon which the implementation of policy is based. If the bureaucracy is very powerful in itself or if state policy is complex and there are no other national organizations concerned with a particular policy area, it may also provide most or all of the information upon which the formulation of that policy rests. Venezuelan bureaucratic organizations during the period under discussion, however, were much closer to the minimum power levels than the maximum, partly because political and economic power was dispersed among the regional caudillos and partly because basic change was never a policy of the governments of the period. As long as government was seen primarily as the maintenance of the nation rather than as the regulator or initiator of change, the bureaucracy could hardly have a monopoly of relevant information.

There was enough necessary information peculiar to the bureaucracy, however, to ensure the importance of a continuing bureaucratic apparatus to the government. From the individual governmental organization's point of view some measure of independence from the regime in power was necessary if it was to continue to function at all, since unlimited patronage privileges held by an outside source could destroy it. Both organizational survival and any desire to fulfill manifest goals operate to reinforce the organization's felt need for autonomy from the regime. While this autonomy may function to provide stability and at least a minimum fulfillment of manifest goals during periods of presidential instability, it is clear that attempts at reform of the system will also be impeded. That is, bureaucratic independence functions to resist changes originating outside the organization. Whether those changes would be good or bad in terms of efficient administration is not as important as their source in this context. Moreover, "reform" has always been the slogan of those who would change governmental organizations, and given Venezuela's political history, it is only natural that this slogan will be received with more than a little skepticism by those who are to be reformed.

Many writers, Groves perhaps paramount among them in a specifically administrative context, have dismissed the Venezuelan public service before 1935 as so weak that it was incapable of defending itself against the executive offices and therefore not important to the later development of the bureaucracy. While it was generally not capable of defending specific individuals, I feel it is a mistake to argue from this that it had no organizational integrity or independence. Control of information alone would ensure its survival, and all available information points to a relative security of the personnel within the system. Even the incident Groves cites as damning evidence of the public services' weakness tends to support this view. He relates the story (possibly apocryphal but by no means improbable) of the prefect to whom Gómez had assigned an illiterate secretary. The prefect complained about this state of affairs to Gómez, who responded by making the secretary the prefect and the ex-prefect the secretary.[5] The point is not that the prefect lost his position but that he was retained in the office in a position that practically ensured he would continue to run it and very probably to make most of the decisions in it. This is more an example of organizational continuity than of personal insecurity.

With the discovery of oil Venezuela embarked upon a course that was to change its society and to alter the culture of which its political system was an integral part. In the short run Gómez, who presided over this early oil period, prevented any major cultural changes. Until his death in 1935 the oil revenues were used primarily for the maintenance of the traditional culture and of Gómez, a traditional caudillo. The nature of the oil industry lent itself to this use, for it employed relatively few people and shipped its products out of the country. The main effect it had on Venezuela was a major increase in governmental revenues that did not involve internal taxation, a situation that could only increase the power of the dictator.

Gómez did, however, have a major effect upon the bureaucracy during his twenty-seven years in power, primarily through making the formal centralization of power effective. The new military roads and improved communications allowed the further development of the bureaucratic centralism traditional in Hispanic cultures, with the result that by 1935 governmental organizations were both formally and actually highly centralized. All authority emanated from the capital, a situation resulting in painfully slow services in the interior. As long as the nation was not changing in any fundamental way, long delays and inefficient procedures could be endured, especially since the slow and uncertain communications system permitted a less than strict application of the rules in special cases. As Venezuela has become more and more attuned to change and an increased tempo of life and as communications have permitted stricter and stricter applications of the rules, bureaucratic centralism has become more and more stringent.

Insofar as any single factor has caused the change in Venezuelan life, that factor has been oil. The long-term result of the discovery of oil has been the conversion of Venezuela from a country whose wealth was derived from the soil to one in which it is derived from the subsoil, a change that could not in itself be termed "development." In the period after 1935 most major landowners either converted to commercial, technologically advanced agriculture or abandoned agriculture and lived upon income derived, either directly or indirectly, from oil.

The result for most farm workers was that the old hacienda pattern of living was broken and a new life had to be fashioned. Subsistence farmers found themselves in an analogous situation because of improved communications and the increased prosperity of the cities, although here the case was more one of attraction to a new life than forced expulsion from the old. The hand-to-mouth existence led by most country people had always been marginal: disease, hunger, and physical discomfort are never attractive to those who must endure them. With the opening of the roads great numbers migrated to the urban centers. The basic culture of the country, based upon the hacienda and an unquestioning acceptance of an unchanging world, began to change under the impact of a technology in which change was essential to life. While the new technology was inherent in the gasoline engines, the telephone and telegraph, and the construction machines and techniques used in the 1930s, it had its greatest impact on Venezuelans in the late 1940s and 1950s. Oil revenues had gone up sharply during the war and the three-year government of popularly based political parties from 1945 to 1948 began public spending programs that the subsequent dictatorship felt compelled to continue and in some cases to expand.[6] While many of the welfare policies of these governments can best be seen as the replacement by the state of the traditional patrón lost by the working man when he left the farm, the technology that enabled the government to implement such large programs, as well as the increased tempo of the 1950s, contributed to the impact of a technology based upon machinery on a population accustomed to the rhythms of nonmechanized agriculture.

The increased revenue and the impact of technological changes were felt in the government as well as in the culture of Venezuela. From a structural viewpoint, the main result was a phenomenal increase in the number of nonministerial organizations. The ministries themselves grew from eight in 1930 to thirteen (Health and Welfare, 1936; Communications, 1936; Labor, 1945; Justice, 1950; and Hydrocarbons and Mines, 1950). All except Justice came either directly or indirectly from the Ministry of Development, so the pattern of ministerial development evident before 1930 was unchanged.

What was definitely an innovation was the increased use of nonministerial organizations. Of the seventy-six that existed in 1972 only two (both development banks) predated 1937. All the rest had been created since then, 89 percent having been created after 1945.[7] The process has continued at a slower rate up to the present date (1976).

A priori, there are three reasons for change-oriented governments to create nonministerial organizations. First, they offer more financial flexibility than ministries, since their charters may be written so that they may accept private investment and maintain independent investment policies of their own. Second, they offer more managerial flexibility, particularly in the management of personnel. And third, the opportunity to remove the new agency from "politics" by placing it outside the traditional patronage domains of the ministries may seem attractive to reform-minded governments. This last is, of course, the obverse of the opportunity to create new patronage domains not under the control of the older organizations. On the other hand, the problem of how to invest the large governmental revenues derived from the oil is by itself a major factor in explaining the ever-increasing use of autonomous and semiautonomous institutions.

The trend towards autonomous institutions has been remarkably steady since 1945, despite radical changes in the form of government. This period covers the reforms of the Trienio (1945–48), the military junta that seized power in 1948, the dictatorship of Pérez Jiménez from 1950 to 1958, and the democratic governments since 1958. Indeed, of the seventy-six existing in 1972 half had been created since 1958.

There had, however, been a change in the nature of the institutions created. During the dictatorship emphasis was placed upon national services (e.g., CANTV, the national telecommunications corporation; CAVN, the national steamship line; and CONAHOTU, the national tourist hotels), whereas from 1958 to 1972 regional and national development organizations accounted for twenty-eight of the thirty-three created.

As has been shown, autonomous organizations have many attractions when considered individually. When they become numerous they also have serious drawbacks. First, and most obviously, their direct accountability only to the president leads to problems of span of control with its corollary of a functional lack of continuing control. Second, the new agencies have the same reasons as the older agencies for desiring as much autonomy from the "meddling" of the central authority as possible. These two factors are mutually reinforcing and together constitute a serious tendency towards bureaucratic anarchy.

III.

BUREAUCRATIC ACCOUNTABILITY

Given the factors supporting agency autonomy noted above, it is clear that accountability is a major issue in the public administration, particularly in view of the proliferation of autonomous corporations. In many ways this is a new focus on the older problem of control in implementation. This is so because with the increased tempo of change in Venezuela and its initiation and direction by the government, the actual implementation of policy has become much more important. The colonial situation had placed a premium on formal acceptance of the regime, often to the detriment of the execution of the laws. This situation has altered to such an extent that change and development have become the primary overt goals of the government. The main focus is now upon the effective execution of the development policies, and the question of control has become a major issue. In my judgment the most effective control over the implementation of national policy by the bureaucracy is exercised not by the agencies themselves but by the political parties. That is, the system of political influence described in the first chapter of this book is essential if the Venezuelan bureaucracy is to function effectively for development goals. This would vary from agency to agency, of course, but if it is accepted that a fundamental goal of democratic Venezuela is the improvement of the conditions of life for most of its people, then the close grass roots "supervision" of the implementation is necessary. Even those agencies primarily engaged in the production rather than the distribution of wealth are positively affected by this criterion, as we shall see in the case of the Guayana Corporation.

Theoretically, the accountability of a bureaucracy is the primary factor in determining whether or not it fulfills its manifest goals. Governmental organizations perform multiple functions, only one of which is the implementation of stated policy. The others, generally termed "latent" functions, are such things as the employment of an organization's members (i.e., the distribution of wealth to its members); the political support of these people to the organization and, usually, to the government; the support of bureaucratic personnel to the political system and to its constituent parts, the parties; the symbolic importance of agencies dedicated to the well-being of the nation or of needy groups within it; and the use of ministries as a "share" in the government for the parties involved in a coalition government or for factions within a majority party or dictatorial regime.

While all these latent functions may be legitimate in terms of the political necessities that ensure their survival, it is clear that they can easily have effects contrary to the manifest goals of any particular agency. Indeed, given the strength of some of these factors it is entirely possible that agencies could survive and prosper without effectively implementing their manifest goals at all.

As a countervailing force there is generally a certain minimum efficacy required of a governmental bureaucracy without which the passage of legislation or the promulgation of presidential decrees become farcical. While one or two agencies may have no manifest output without seriously discommoding the regime in power, if a great many of them have no manifest output the government becomes unable to act. When this occurs a serious national crisis usually results.

This can be cold comfort for the majority of the population, however, for there is nothing to guarantee that any subsequent regime will press any harder for the effective implementation of policy affecting them. Governments have historically been accountable mainly to the producers of wealth, not to the potential users of that wealth. The situation that existed during the Pérez Jiménez years was precisely this, with the proviso that the producers of wealth were the foreign oil companies.

The great achievement of the subsequent democratic governments of Venezuela has been to provide a system of accountability that does not depend upon the bureaucracy itself for information and the generation of policy. Multiparty systems are not the only forms of government that can function effectively for the change and national development that benefit the masses of the people. Cuba, Peru, and Mexico are cases in point, but all of these systems depend upon one basic condition in order to function: the political organization of the mass of the people is a fundamental prerequisite if reform and development are to take place. In Venezuela since 1958 this has taken the form of a commitment to democratic process and the organization of free mass-based parties. Powell argues persuasively that the basic relation between party leaders and the rank and file members is that of patron to client.[1] The important thing from our perspective is that this relation is a reciprocal one: the patron must be of value to the client and deliver at least minimum benefits to him or the client will find another patron. Since alternative parties are available in Venezuela this provides the parties with powerful motives for delivering their promises. That the patron/client relationship is inherently unequal, with the weight of power and influence clearly on the side of the patron, is an inherent danger of this system. It is always possible that the party hierarchy will find it more comfortable to engage in elite rather than mass politics, and the basic relationship of rank and file to leaders would degenerate into the vote connection only. That is, the direct and personal reciprocal nature of the system would be lost.

Given the importance of personal contacts at all levels in Venezuela and the consequent conviction that it is only through personal ties that benefits can be expected, this loss of the personal element in party life would most probably result in a great diminution of political activity by the mass of the Venezuelan people. The effect on the bureaucracy would be to remove one of the greatest pressures for the effective implementation of policy that exists in Venezuela: the political pressure from the parties generated by their need to deliver benefits to their members.

It is not disputed here that this method of ensuring bureaucratic performance is unequal and biased implementation. It implies that "nonpolitical" Venezuelans are not very likely to gain the benefits of laws passed on a formally universalistic basis. The system is hardly perfect, but over the last sixteen years it has benefited the mass of Venezuelans more than any of the previous arrangements.

Certainly under the Pérez Jiménez regime what little was done for the common people was done under the pressure of the clandestine party activity of Acción Democrática. Moreover, the public housing that was the main effort of the regime in this direction was largely of the "vertical slum" variety, often resulting in conditions nearly as bad as those it replaced. We have had experience with this type of urban renewal in the United States. The experiences seem to be parallel both in their results and in the elitist and non-reciprocal nature of the politics involved.

It may be argued that under both Pérez Jiménez and the democratic regimes the bureaucracy was used more for its symbolic value than for actual development. Certainly the explosive expansion of the school system was undertaken for reasons as symbolic as they were educational. The ministry and the party elite were both perfectly aware that the quality of education would be very poor for a relatively long time, and that the consequences for the nation of the creation of a large number of inadequately educated degree holders would be negative. On the other hand, the expansion was clearly one desired by most people, and the opportunity to upgrade teachers and students, if taken advantage of, could gradually alleviate the situation. It is problematic whether or not a more elitist and gradual expansion of education would have resulted in a more positive outcome, since it never occurred. The present situation is one that results in continuous and strong pressure on the parties to provide better education to the children of their members. Because something has been delivered there is increased pressure for more.

A second symbolic effort of the new regimes was and is land reform. It has been argued that the Venezuelan land reform program has benefited mainly local party leaders and that the goal of many small, family owned and operated farms has not been reached.[2] That is, the program has been responsive to particularistic, party pressures rather than to the universalistic, humanistic goals written into the law. On the other hand, the program has resulted in a much more widespread distribution of wealth and land than would have been the case without it. There is no compelling reason to believe that without party pressures and the necessity to deliver on the patron/client relation, the reform would have been effective at all.

The mixture of symbolic and real policy implementation evident in the two examples above is, of course, present in any governmental action. Politics deals in symbols in any political system. I am arguing that in Venezuela the bureaucratic implementation of law would be far more symbolic than it is were it not for the political pressure on the parties to benefit their members. Moreover, traditional culture supports symbolic rather than "real" policies.

Patronage, endemic in the Venezuelan system, is a natural result of the patron/client nature of the parties. Surely the most direct and easiest way to benefit a client is to get him a government job. This requires no great change in the social or economic culture of the country and results in immediate real benefits to the client.

Insofar as clients are unqualified for their positions in the bureaucracy or unnecessary positions must be created for them, this can only have negative effects upon the agencies' efficiency. A system of attainment has developed, however, that combines achievement and party status considerations.[3] Under this system employees are chosen on the basis of party membership and professional qualifications. Laborers, a large and unskilled category, are generally chosen solely on the basis of party qualifications, although this situation is mitigated by the patron/client relationships that develop within agencies, particularly those that have managed to maintain a substantial degree of independence. On the whole, the highest and lowest levels of the bureaucracy are most vulnerable to patronage pressures. Middle level staff such as the secretary in Groves's story are generally retained, although their titles may change. In large measure they provide the continuity and knowledge upon which bureaucratic effectiveness is based.

Bureaucratic Strategies

The object of most bureaucratic strategies is, of course, agency autonomy. Among other things, bureaucratic independence cuts to a minimum the patronage that must be met, isolates the agency from the problems of other agencies as well as removing it from the day-to-day supervision of the parties, permits the agency better control of information about the agency, removes competing patron/client networks from management, and generally makes the internal management problems less complex. One great advantage in external relations is that a nonpartisan image can reinforce the idea that the agency is fundamentally "national" in its focus rather than "political."

On the negative side, agency autonomy as such removes a great deal of the necessity to produce, tends to focus agency attention upon latent goals, makes coordination with other agencies difficult (especially if they are also autonomous), makes the national coordination of policy more difficult, and makes comprehensive reform impossible. Moreover, the scope for bad leadership as well as for good is amplified, along with the increased possibility that the rosca system will degenerate into simple internal patronage.

The negative aspects of autonomy seem to have been rather important during the Pérez Jiménez period. Many of the autonomous agencies created then tended to function for the enrichment of their members rather than for the implementation of their manifest goals. In the absence of a developed and legitimate party system to provide alternate lines of communication and pressure, this sort of thing was very difficult to stop. The record shows that Pérez Jiménez did not put much effort into its curtailment.

The positive aspects of autonomy have been obvious to bureaucrats in every administrative system, but the colonial heritage made them especially possible in Venezuela. The parallel and overlapping organizations of the Spanish administration depended upon relative autonomy for their continued existence, and the king and the council were careful to maintain the separate and independent status of each of the elements under them. The practice has continued in Venezuela to such an extent that Hanson was able to find exact counterparts for them in the Ministry of Education.[4] In particular, the use of inspectors attached directly to the minister who have the authority to jump the entire hierarchy is of interest. Such a system combines checks and balances with the personal basis of authority noted above.

On a national scale the independence of each agency is limited in part by the practice of requiring multiple check-offs with other agencies. For example, if Education wishes to build a school it must first gain the agreement of Public Works, which will do the actual building, and of the national planning agency (CORDIPLAN). One effect is that any substantial disagreement will be referred to the president for his decision.

For those agencies in a position to employ it, the appeal to technological necessities is a highly rewarding one. In essence this strategy dictates a proven effectiveness in a technological field, a national consensus that the work of the agency is very important to the nation, and an ability to avoid becoming closely involved with programs directly involving large numbers of people. This last is necessary if political pressures generated by the needs of these people are to be avoided. The foremost practitioner of this strategy in Venezuelan has been the Venezuelan Guayana Corporation (CVG).[5]

The CVG is a descendant of a commission set up in 1953 to study the possibilities for developing the hydroelectric potential of the Caroní river. At the same time an office was established to develop

an iron and steel mill in the same area. This latter office established
a truly remarkable record for peculation and for ineffectiveness at
everything else. The hydroelectric commission had in the mean-
while established itself as technologically proficient and in 1960
was called in to pick up the pieces. The result has been impressive:
all of the CVG's major goals have been accomplished and new
ones set and achieved.

Since its inception the CVG has followed a policy of not becoming involved with policies entailing short-range provision of education, health facilities, welfare, or anything else that would have
required interaction with large numbers of needy people. While
employees of the industries operating under the CVG's aegis were
provided these services by the industrial corporation involved
(whether these corporations were national or foreign), large numbers of needy citizens have not had benefits.

The factors that enabled the CVG to pursue such a policy, however, emphasize the difficulties facing other agencies attempting
to employ the same strategy. First, the area in which the CVG
operates was and is relatively uninhabited. From the outset the
CVG was free of the need to respond to the political pressures
generated by the unemployed and the needy. Also, the types of
industries they were creating did not exist in Venezuela, so they
did not suffer from the political pressures that might have been
generated by competing businesses. That more people have not
come to the Guayana has been due to a combination of the CVG's
policies and the checks and balances system of agency responsibility. The charter of the CVG was written very broadly, providing authority and responsibility for the welfare of all the people
of the Guayana. At the same time, the more traditional ministries
(Education, Health and Welfare, Labor, Children's Council, etc.)
and agencies involved with social policy were also responsible for
the area. Not surprisingly, they left the sparsely settled region up
to the CVG. Hard pressed to respond to the demands generated in
the heavily populated parts of the nation, they were not eager to
make major investments in an area in which another agency had
equally good jurisdiction. The result has been to delimit an area
in which industrial and infrastructure development has been sepa-
rated from short-range social responsibilities. Venezuelan workers are acutely aware that while skilled work is available in the
Guayana, support for those unable to get jobs is small or non-

existent. Since they do not live in that area in the first place and welfare agencies do operate where they are living, there has been no mass movement to Ciudad Guayana. It is important to note that if the other agencies of government were not operating in the traditionally settled areas of the country, the CVG strategy probably would not work.

At the same time, it is of great interest from an administrative point of view that the strategy depends upon technological proficiency and the ability to deliver upon the promises of production. With the introduction of mass political organizations the budget comes under intense scrutiny. A large operation that could not or did not deliver its promises and simultaneously did not provide benefits to parties through its latent functions would have a very difficult time surviving. The petrochemical plant in Morón may be taken as a case in point. Here there have been great difficulties in production, and the agency has had to fight for appropriations and at times for its existence.

The division that CVG leaders have successfully made has been between the functions of production and distribution. By stressing their technological competence at production and exploiting the CVG's location they have managed to retain their formal independence and respected position. While its location has not been available to other agencies, the basic appeal to technical proficiency and competence has been made with some success. CADAFE, for example, the national agency responsible for generating and distributing electrical power, has a good reputation based upon its performance and has rarely become the focus of political controversy. INOS, the water and sanitation agency, is frequently embroiled in controversy over sewers and somewhat less so over water. Public Works is even more exposed, primarily because it is responsible for almost all public construction in the country and partly because of the large numbers of people it employs. Health and Welfare probably comes in for more criticism than any agency except Education. The situation is such that self-fulfilling prophecies work against the agency, as in the case of public hospitals. Poor Venezuelans generally tend to view a hospital as a place to die. Consequently, they rarely enter one before they are very seriously ill. That the Health and Welfare hospitals are generally crowded and the staff overworked does not help the situation.

Even so, the appeal to "technical" norms is engaged in by all agencies. This is, of course, an appeal to the professional standards and achievement norms dear to the heart of any administrative reformer, and as such is always sure of a hearing. It tends to be successful in direct relation to the degree to which the agency can disassociate itself from people. This is why Education can scarcely expect its appeals to academic standards materially to lessen the political pressure brought to bear upon it. The ministry can hardly disassociate itself from either its actual or its potential students, just as Health and Welfare cannot disassociate itself from those people who die in its hospitals, even though many of them may have waited far too long before entering.

The appeal to the "uncultured" or "uneducated" nature of the clientele is in itself a bureaucratic ploy, although it is much less successful than the appeal to technology. It is not likely to be very effective in warding off criticism and outside interference in the agencies' affairs when those same agencies are responsible for improving the culture and education of the populace. Generally speaking, it is a dangerous tactic capable of boomeranging on the agency, and is consequently used very sparingly.

A third strategy that might be mentioned is concealment—if no one knows what you're doing they can hardly criticize you for it. This is likewise limited by the amount of contact the agency has with people and has the drawback of reducing the agency's likelihood of increased funding. Insofar as it is successful, it depends upon ties with high government officials willing to defend the agency in private. While fairly common during the Pérez Jiménez years, it is rarely used today.

Finally, the appeal to national need is an obvious strategy. Most effective when combined with a reputation for competence, it is nevertheless used by all agencies. It has its strongest political appeal in precisely those areas in which bureaucratic action is most difficult, that of "people" problems. Cultural and economic transitions have both created and exposed needs that, given the patron/client political culture, the government is expected to meet.

The most interesting observation to be made on the strategies discussed here is that they tend to be successful only if the agency is widely known to be technically proficient. That is, the present system on at least a macroscopic basis tends to reinforce achievement, or rather, the reputation for efficacy. This qualification points up the desirability of some means of checking on the actual production of the government bureaucracy. Given Venezuelan society and the history of the bureaucracy, 'this observer believes the only system strong enough to maintain this pressure for achievement is the political party system, and that only as long as strong and vigorous mass party organizations are maintained. Such a system clearly results in an unjust situation for nonpartisan citizens and varying degrees of reward for those in weak parties, but it has resulted in more benefits for more people than any previous Venezuelan system. Whether or not it is more beneficial than nondemocratic socialist systems is a moot point and beyond the scope of this paper. Certainly the costs as well as the benefits of the two systems can and usually do differ radically.

IV.

REFORM

While it may be argued that the Venezuelan bureaucracy is functioning more in the interests of most Venezuelans now than it has in the past, no one claims that it has reached perfection or, in the eyes of some observers, even an adequate level of competence. The previous discussion has sought to point out that any such blanket claims about the bureaucracy are difficult to defend. Some agencies are very good and some are rather spectacularly not so. During the Pérez Jiménez years the bureaucracy both expanded enormously and gained a reputation for corruption and inefficiency that in some cases was probably undeserved. At the least during those years the main motivation for efficient and effective achievement of overt goals must have been the dedication and conscience of the bureaucrats involved. The support such men and women received was by all accounts minimal.

With the institution of democratic government, the problem of administrative reform was approached from two directions. First, attempts were made to improve the "coordination" of programs. This was and is an attempt to reduce the independence of the bureaucratic organizations and reduce the overlapping and conflicting programs resulting from this independence. There is also, of course, an attempt to increase the regime's control over these agencies. Second, there have been efforts to effect an internal reform of the bureaucracy, centering upon the traditional areas of organization, methods and personnel.

The main strategy for reform was dictated by the nature of the administrative system itself. The one office in the nation that combined both authority and the personal attributes necessary to command respect was that of the presidency. Consequently, it is not surprising that the main attempt to reform the administrative system was located in that office. State governments, which might have been given increased authority both to determine their own needs and to coordinate the activities of national agencies, were apparently not seriously considered as the locus of this action. The reasons are not different to ascertain: the only sources for the authority of governors are the national parties and the president. Since the ministries and heads of autonomous agencies generally have both more physical resources and more prestige than the governors and have equally strong if not stronger personal ties to the president, such a course would have only added to the pressures upon the presidency.

CORDIPLAN, the office of coordination and planning set up in the presidency in 1958, was designed to provide the president and the nation with (1) long-range national planning designed to set priorities and allocate resources so that national goals could be formulated and met, and (2) a mechanism through which the work of bureaucratic organizations could be effectively coordinated.[1] The first mission has been met through the development and publication of four-year plans in the context of long term goals, the second through the requirement that all major projects of the agencies must have clearance from CORDIPLAN before they can be implemented.

The effectiveness of CORDIPLAN is clearly contingent upon the president's continued support. It is unlikely that demands on the presidency will be channeled through CORDIPLAN unless the president forcefully insists upon it, and the requirement for its approval of programs can be easily overridden by an appeal to the president. Its history to date has been mixed. President Betancourt (Rómulo Betancourt, president, 1959–63) made extensive use of CORDIPLAN; President Leoni (Raul Leoni, president 1964–68) somewhat less, and President Caldera (Rafael Caldera, president, 1969–73) less still. President Pérez (Carlos Andrés Pérez, president, 1974–) has given indications that he will rely heavily on the agency, but at this writing it is too early to evaluate the situation.

The long-range planning that CORDIPLAN has done has been effective in that perspective has been given to national goals, and the consequences of these goals have been spelled out. On the other hand, the predictions CORDIPLAN has made have been less than totally accurate and, as implied above, its control over the bureaucracy less than complete. It can best understood as a planning agency attached to an executive with many other pressures upon him. As such it is only one input into decision making and cannot be expected to formulate definitive plans or to have the power to carry them out.

Probably because of the success of the CVG the Caldera government in 1969 set up a system of regions through which the national agencies would have to channel their efforts. As noted earlier, the effect this has had on administrative practices has been minimal. Insofar as this system has potential it rests with the establishment of planning and decision-making staff in the regional headquarters. This is obviously an effort to wrest complete control from the Caracas headquarters and disperse it to the interior. For the reasons already discussed, it is unlikely to work without major and continuous support from the presidency. Again, it is too early to say what effect the Pérez presidency will have on the regional "headquarters."

Regional development corporations modeled on the CVG have also been set up. Because of the differing demographic conditions and the already existing commercial and industrial establishments in these regions, however, it is highly unlikely that they will be able to reproduce the CVG's performance. They may be developed into effective planning and investment organizations, but it is doubtful that the experience of the CVG will be helpful to them in this development. The strategies and techniques developed by the CVG are not viable options for them, tailored as they are to empty regions and single-agency dominance.

Within the last few years most of the autonomous agencies have been formally assigned to the appropriate ministries. While the CVG managed to retain its position in the president's office, the net effect has been to raise the status of the ministers and to reduce the workload of the president. It is to be hoped that this delegation of authority will spread, but the likelihood that this will take place is small.

The logical end of decentralization is independent local governments, but this is very unlikely in Venezuela. In the colonial period local governments were legally nil except in times of crisis. Even so, they provided the only governmental posts that could be held by those born in the Americas, and as such became the focus of "national" politics. Most of the political movements during the independence movement were derived from municipal councils. Since then they have receded in importance, but their ties with the community have remained. In Venezuela this is complicated by the method of election. Elections are held every five years for all elective offices in the country, and each voter casts only two ballots: one for the president and another for a party. Although these are computed for states and municipalities, the effect is to determine local representation by national issues.

Municipal government is consistent with the rest of the Venezuelan system in that it has legal jurisdiction over a broad area, including schools, water and sewers, zoning, housing, etc. These areas are also the responsibilities of national agencies, of course, so the pattern of overlapping jurisdictions and responsibilities is repeated at the local level. Given their legal jurisdiction and the fact that in Venezuela local governments control their hinterlands (the county/town distinctions that are proving so troublesome in the United States have never existed in Venezuela) local government is a logical focus of coordination. Moreover, these governmental units are intimately connected with the actual implementation of policy and can therefore be expected to be more aware of immediate needs and problems than those organizations that are centered in Caracas.

Local governments in Venezuela have very little income, however, and have thus not been in a position to influence the actions of the national agencies. The traditions of national patron/client political relations and small financial resources have combined to perpetuate the weak position of local governments.

The focus of local government as a means of improving the performance of national agencies and contributing to Venezuela's development was noted in Caracas, however, and in 1962 the Betancourt government created FUNDACOMUN, an autonomous government corporation responsible for the professionalization and development of local government.[2] Acting with the support of the Institute of Public Administration and other North American foundations, FUNDACOMUN has done much to increase the income of local governments and demonstrate their feasibility as strong actors in coordinating and planning local development. Incomes have been increased through the rationalization and professional collection of local taxes that have historically been reserved to the cities but generally not efficiently or systematically used. Unfortunately, national elections cannot be considered proper vehicles for local issues. The changes in town councils resulting from them have tended to vitiate local effectiveness. On the other hand, the increased town finances have made the town councils more important, and with increasing professionalization of council staffs, the councils themselves can be expected to take more aggressive stands on local issues.

Interestingly enough, it is the overlapping nature of agency responsibilities that gives these local governments their best chance
for effective work. In the Guayana the town council of San Felix,
the existing municipal government for the region which has become Ciudád Guayana, has been unable to influence the CVG in
any meaningful way or to function effectively to represent local
needs. As Peattie and others have pointed out, local inhabitants
who are not employed by the government or the new business
corporations are in many ways worse off than their peers in other
parts of the country.[3] Because of the CVG's effective hegemony
over the area, local government there is ineffective as a separate
authority.

The most successful local government in Venezuela outside Caracas is that of Valencia, located in the heart of traditional Venezuela. With relatively dense population patterns and a thriving
commercial and industrial population Valencia's town council has
managed effectively to influence national agencies and to plan for
the development of the town. As long as the town council itself
remained united and aggressive, the agencies working in the area
proved both willing and able to work with it. Indeed, in some cases
the town council provided additional support to line personnel in
dealing with their Caracas office. The election in 1969 split the
council to such a degree that it became largely ineffective in this
role. Nevertheless, the possibilities for effective local government
had been shown to exist. With FUNDACOMUN's continued activity in the field it is likely that this method of coordinating and
planning the actions of national agencies will increase in importance, as will the possibilities of independent action by the municipalities.

Institutional Reform

With the fall of Pérez Jiménez it became possible to act upon the
common knowledge that the Venezuelan bureaucracy was something less than perfect.

The commission for administrative reform set up by the pro-
visional junta in May 1958 had been recommended by Herbert
Emmerich, a senior consultant of the United Nations Public Administration Division.[4] Emmerich had been asked by the junta to

advise them on the course they might take in reforming the bureaucracy, which seemed in obvious need of such an effort after eight years of Pérez Jiménez. He proposed the creation of a "Hoover Commission" that would concentrate upon organization and personnel policies.

This new agency, the Public Administration Commission (CAP), was by no means faced with a simple problem. In addition to whatever weaknesses existed in the bureaucracy, its position as an agency placed it in opposition to the established agencies, both ministerial and autonomous. Whatever recommendations it might make towards a lessening of bureaucratic independence were further compromised by the fact that it was itself an independent agency that reported directly to the president. The situation was one that obviously required delicacy and tact if progress was to be made.

One of the first acts of the commission, however, was to contract with three United States firms for professional help in investigating the bureaucracy and in formulating the commission's recommendations. Given the close identification of Pérez Jiménez and the United States within Venezuela[5] this could hardly be called tactful. The recommendations made were also far from delicate: the commission called for a reorganization of the entire bureaucracy, the full application of the merit system of recruitment and promotion, a position classification plan, and a uniform compensation plan. The first request attacked institutions from above and the others from below: reorganization would lessen or abolish hard-won formal independence, and the Weberian personnel policies would weaken if not destroy the traditional system of personal authority and loyalty that held them together. It is not surprising that the commission's recommendations were not implemented.

Given the situation in which the new government found itself (and for which it had been preparing since 1948), what is surprising is that the commission received as much support as it did. Acción Democrática, the leading reform party in Venezuela, had returned from exile and won the 1958 elections with a majority. Committed to a fully participatory democratic process and extensive reforms centering upon the use of the oil revenues for the good of all the regions and citizens of Venezuela, the government soon found itself the target of armed resistance from both the left and the right. Struggling to institute and strengthen the myriad institutions necessary for its vision to be realized, it was in no position to alienate public bureaucrats, the only possible instrument for implementing these plans. The army was obviously sacrosanct, if only because its neutrality at the least was necessary for the government's continued existence. The quick defeats of two military units that rebelled against the government in 1962 by forces loyal to the government demonstrated the wisdom of this policy.

The regime itself, then, did not have a free hand with the reform of the bureaucracy. To take an extreme example, a thoroughgoing purge of "inefficient" governmental employees has often been recommended (usually by foreign experts) but never carried out. Given the above analysis, the reasons for the nonimplementation are obvious. It would be both too political, because the inevitable result would be the firing of large groups of persons active within particular parties, and not political enough in the sense that a direct result would be the creation of a large class of impoverished people almost certainly alienated from the political system responsible for their situation. A well-developed country with a large number of jobs in nongovernmental organizations could absorb such a blow only with difficulty. Venezuela, a developing nation in which the government directly or indirectly provides for most of the people, could obviously not contemplate such a drastic method of reform.

To say that the reformer is limited to less drastic reforms is to say that he must balance the requirements of the manifest and latent functions of agencies. Within these limitations he is presented with two broad strategies: (1) a concentration upon the implementation of policy in an attempt to make it more efficacious or (2) a concentration upon the instrument of policy implementation, that is, the agency itself. While these two approaches are not contradictory, they do seem to be contrary. A preoccupation with efficacy will generally lead to inefficiency, or will at least not be overly concerned with existing inefficiencies, while a bureaucratic reformer may well lose sight of the output of an agency as he labors to rationalize its structure and personnel policies. The regime solved this problem by setting up different organizations for the different approaches, CORDIPLAN and FUNDACOMUN on the external side and CAP for internal reforms.

A further decision facing reform planners is whether to concentrate their efforts where they will be best received or where they are most needed. Those organizations most susceptible to reform are usually those that are already fairly efficient and rational. That is, they are organizations that already accept efficiency, rationality, and other reform criteria as relevant and necessary. On the other hand, inefficient and "irrational" organizations primarily concerned with fulfilling latent functions are unlikely to be receptive to these ideas, no matter how important their manifest functions in terms of national priorities. Such an organization might support a program of increased efficacy while denying the validity of efficiency criteria. This would reinforce a situation contrary to the goals of institutional reform. To work with the agency in an attempt to reform it, in its turn, would seem to displace effort from the efficacious implementation of policy to the reform of the institution, and as such is contrary to the efficacy criteria of the first strategy of reform.

Given the tension between efficiency and efficacy strategies it seems inevitable that national policy will incline towards one or the other. For the agency of administrative reform, however, it is most likely that the main stress will be upon efficiency and institutional reform. This is so because the agency's own manifest goal is the reform of the bureaucracy and not the implementation of policy, which remains with the existing bureaucracy. At the same time the manifest goal of the regime in power is the implementation of its programs. It seems inevitable that there will be tension between any government and its agency of internal administrative reform.

The obvious implication is that the deep and thoroughgoing administrative reform recommended by the commission, however desirable for the efficient implementation of manifest governmental goals, was not a political possibility. The Betancourt government continued to fund the commission at a high level but did not press for the passage of enabling legislation that would have legalized the imposition of reforms.

CAP, initially under the guidance of its United States advisors and afterwards under personnel they had trained, continued to advocate major reforms. Its effort during this initial period (1958–62) was to prepare job classifications, pay scales, entering examinations, and promotion schedules that would constitute the new criteria for personnel administration.

In 1963, disappointed in their plans to reform the entire bureaucracy, the commission's leaders decided to concentrate upon advising those organizations within the government that had been the most receptive to their ideas on reform. In doing so they abandoned, at least temporarily, any idea of a massive structural reorganization in favor of a concentration upon personnel, budgeting, and management procedures withing the self-selected target institutions.

Training, initiated in the National School of Public Administration (ENAP, a part of the commission created in 1963) was concentrated upon low-level personnel, with most of the courses on a high school or, at most, a junior college level. The relatively low level involved would indicate that even the self-selected institutions were wary of any changes in their internal authority structures. That is, they desired more efficient work by lower level personnel but did not want any change in the way their organizations were run.

This situation continued during the Leoni administration (1963–68). While the commission's placement close to the president undoubtedly invested it with the president's prestige, it also ensured his close control of its activities, an effect that could hardly have been accidental. Small and controversial, the new commission did not have the bureaucratic capital that would have permitted independent action. The prestige of the agency was maintained, as was a relatively high level of funding, but necessary legislation was not passed. If the commission was to have any impact at all it would have to obtain the support of at least some of the older and stronger organizations.

A few of these organizations were interested, but even these were careful to preserve their independence and proved reluctant to abandon the systems of personal loyalty, strongly authoritarian leadership styles, and centralism within the organization that had (at least in the eyes of those most directly involved) served in ensuring organizational and personal survival for so long.

By the time Rafael Caldera was inaugurated the situation had changed, primarily because of the continuation of participatory democracy and the lessening of violent opposition. Through the survival of the democratic system, elected governments possessed more latitude in 1969 than in 1959 because of the increased legitimacy provided by ten years of democracy. Moreover, the nation had demonstrated that far-reaching social and economic reforms of benefit to all Venezuelans were possible, a situation that enhanced the power of the government to enact new ones.

Reform measures that in 1959 would have had the effect of freezing a good many of Pérez Jiménez's followers into their jobs now confronted a bureaucracy largely made up of members of the dominant democratic parties. This analysis was shared, apparently, by the COPEI government. Caldera was elected on a reform platform, one plank of which was administrative reform. In this he received the backing in Congress of both his own party and of Acción Democratica, which together formed a majority. The Career Law, first presented in 1961, was passed in 1970. It envisions a comprehensive civil service system providing for such things as recruitment and promotion by examination, uniform pay scales, comprehensive job classifications, vacations with pay, dismissal only for proven cause, and other protections for employees. The Career Law also provides for the creation of the Central Office óf Personnel, which is charged with the development of specific statutes governing the various aspects of the proposed system. The Public Administration Commission itself pressed for a reorganization designed to rationalize the governmental structure, reducing the functional independence of the autonomous agencies as well as reducing their number. As noted above, it was successful in having most autonomous agencies assigned to ministries rather than to the presidency.

In 1969 the new head of the commission insisted upon the relocation of his own agency into CORDIPLAN, the main planning and coordinating agency of the presidency. By giving up the formal privilege of direct access to the presidency, and integrating the commission into the widely respected CORDIPLAN, the influence of the commission for reform has been concentrated in the agency most successful in integrating governmental action. Moreover, a strategy designed to promote and aid reform from within rather than without had been developed. Also in 1969 departments for administrative reform were created by law in all ministries and autonomous organizations. The new offices (called Oficina Central de Reforma Administrativa, OCRA) provide staff input to the executives of their organizations and, presumably, liaison with the commission. As such they provide the commission with at least a foot in the door of any agency. The staffing of these new offices is crucial to any reform effort channeled through them.

Given the change from a massive imposition of reforms to a selective cooperation in reforms, the training function of the commission has become more important, at least from the reformer's point of view. Originally designed to aid low-level bureaucrats in making up education they had missed and thus becoming formally eligible for promotion, the National School of Public Administration (ENAP) has in the last few years emphasized more and more its role as a graduate center for middle and upper level professional administrators. The rationale behind such a change in focus is clear: if administrative reform depends upon the willingness of largely independent organizations to reform themselves, then the personnel within these organizations must be able to understand and sympathize with the goals of reform. More immediately, the personnel of the administrative reform offices within these agencies must understand what administrative reform is all about. The new courses are designed to provide this understanding, and in fact many of their graduates now staff the reform offices.

The northern Inter-American Center for Training in Public Administration of the Organization of American States (CICAP-OEA, *sede norte*) is closely allied with ENAP. CICAP offers graduate level courses in public administration to governmental personnel of the northern Latin American and Caribbean nations. Its offices and Caracas classrooms are located in the commission's offices, and the two schools cooperate closely. Many of ENAP's students participate in CICAP's international courses and some of the courses in ENAP's graduate curriculum are taught by CICAP personnel.

Most of the ministries and agencies have their own training programs. With few exceptions they are concerned with training lower level personnel in technical skills. As such they are unlikely to affect the internal organization or patterns of authority in their agencies, although they undoubtedly contribute to an increased efficiency in particular jobs.[6]

The Faculty of Law in the Central University offers courses in administrative law. Many of their graduates have entered the public services and are often found on the side of reform. The courses themselves, however, are basically limited to a legalistic approach to administrative situations and as such are very much within the traditional mold.

The Institute for Higher Administrative Studies (IESA), located in Caracas, is a private graduate school for public and business administration. It is staffed by individuals (both Venezuelan and foreign) who have earned North American Ph.D.'s or gained the equivalent training elsewhere, and offers a full master's degree program in both fields. Its small size and funding difficulties are negative factors in its influence on administration, but if it survives it could become a major factor in future reforms.

PART II

THE SURVEY

V.

CHANGE AND BUREAUCRATS

The previous section focused on society and public administration. This section will deal with individual members of the Venezuelan bureaucracy and what they think of efficiency and innovation in the public service, personal responsibilities out of it, and what they might do if called to choose between professional and personal values. A final section analyzes responses to questions on some of the strategies available to administrative reformers in Venezuela. Our respondents were the students and alumni of the graduate programs of the National School of Public Administration in 1971. They are not a random sample of the bureaucracy but might be termed "reform bureaucrats" in that they have all studied administrative reform in ENAP. The average time our respondents had spent in the public service was nine years and their average age was thirty-three. Ninety-seven percent held undergraduate degrees and 52 percent were middle level executives at the time of the study. All were Venezuelan civil servants. This last is hardly surprising, since a requirement for entrance into ENAP's graduate programs was recommendation and support from a public agency. From a study population of 291 persons, 153 returned completed questionnaires.

The respondents had wide and diverse experiences in the public service and covered a wide range of jobs and agencies. Eleven of the twelve ministries and twenty-five of seventy-six nonministerial agencies were represented, with the respondents evenly split between the two. About half of the respondents were division or section chiefs, but 10 percent were department heads and 37 percent were professionals with no organizational command responsibilities. Line and staff people were about equal, and one out of four was a woman. "Line" personnel are those engaged in the actual implementation of policy (e.g., a civil engineer engaged in building a road), and staff personnel support line operations (e.g., the accountant who issues pay checks or a civil engineer engaged in planning future roads).

Before discussing the results of the survey it might be helpful to discuss some of the theories about individual bureaucrats that are the bases of our approach. The ultimate goal of behavioral studies such as this one is to learn something about the actual behavior of the respondents. In our case the behavior that interests us is the actual implementation of manifest governmental policies. We would like to know just how efficient and innovative this implementation is and what kind of people within the public service are instrumental in achieving it.

The indirect method we have used in this study suffers from a problem of intuitive assumptions. Assuming that the efficiency and innovation scores derived from the respondents' questionnaires accurately reflect their actual attitudes towards these values, it requires an act of faith to assume that their attitudes have a causal effect upon their actions. Bureaucratic situations may be so constraining that individual administrators have very little freedom to choose among possible alternatives. Poor planning both above and below him, a general atmosphere of unconcern about delays and time in general, excessively rigorous accounting procedures, and the delegation of responsibility for programs without the delegation of the authority to achieve them can hamstring the most energetic and concerned administrator. His attitudes, consequently, may have very little immediate impact upon policy implementation. We do not have data on situational factors for the individual respondents and cannot allow for situations in which these factors differ.

Carried to its logical extreme an argument which stresses situational factors implies that the administrators' attitudes towards the values which interest us in this study are irrelevant in that the administrator cannot in any individual case act upon them. This is, of course, the persistent philosophical question of determinism and free will finding its expression in administrative terms.

If one accepts a deterministic philosophy, then attitudes such as those we are studying are determined by the situations in which the respondents have been required to act, and as such are better seen as consequences of bureaucratic reality than as possible causal factors. If one accepts the opposite view, the same attitudes represent the potential of the respondents for actions in accord with the values measured, and are thus more an indicator of future actions than past situations.

The truth most probably lies between the two extremes. If it is unrealistic to believe that every individual has unlimited freedom of action in every case, it is equally unrealistic to believe that a person's beliefs have no effect upon his actions. Even if actions are severely constrained in particular decisions, it is highly unlikely that an administrator's attitudes and values were not significant factors in the creation of the situations in which he must act. That is, attitudes of an administrator are relevant even if situational factors tend to dominate particular decisions, since unless he has very recently arrived in his position his attitudes have become a part of the situation, particularly as it is seen by his subordinates and (probably to a lesser degree) by his superiors.

The present study is designed to rate the respondents on efficiency and innovation indexes and to relate these to the respondents' backgrounds and opinions on administrative reform strategies. The reader must decide from his own experience the relevance these attitudes and opinions have to the actual implementation of policy.

An analogous debate in the study of public administration is the effect of organizational structure upon administrative behavior and vice versa. The Weberian model posits as an ideal type a deterministic structure: the ideal bureaucracy should be capable of determining the actions of its personnel to such an extent that their attitudes are irrelevant. While Weber recognized that such an ideal could never be fully realized, he believed that it could be approximated closely enough to make it the best model for actual bureaucracies. A very natural consequence of this basic theory was the idea that the public administration is not a policy-making instrument. That is, that the implementation of policy is a mechanical process that does not significantly alter the policy.

The human relations movement in public administration focused attention upon the actual behavior of administrative personnel. Since then it has become generally recognized that the administrative apparatus does have a major impact upon the implementation of policy, especially if the policy runs counter to the values of those who are entrusted with its implementation. It follows that this process will be most visible where governmental policy is concerned with or influenced by major societal changes, for it is in these situations that policy and the public administrator are most likely to clash. It is not surprising that the most complete exposition of this problem is found in the literature of development administration, since the developing nations are those that are most obviously and frequently undergoing deep and traumatic societal changes.

The causal factors of change remain a matter of dispute. It is clear that the example of the industrialized nations and the impact of their products upon the nonindustrialized world is the occasion for change in the latter, but the idea that the latter can or should duplicate the social and political institutions of the western nations is now a matter of dispute. The question of just how and with what institutions the present industrialized nations became so is perhaps an academic question at this point, for it has become apparent that the conditions for change in the contemporary world are radically different from those which confronted Western Europe and North America in the eighteenth and nineteenth centuries. Richard Adams has explored these differences, basing his discussion upon the idea that contemporary nonindustrialized states are now faced with the problems of adapting to a changing world and coping with the conditions created by the technology, products, economies, and foreign relations of the industrialized nations. He terms this process "secondary development" and holds that "a basic characteristic of secondary development is that the government exercises a position of power, allowing it to juggle the factors of development to achieve a social reorganization that will not only permit but also hasten development."[1] He emphasizes the role of the government and the primacy of social innovations by stating that "a cardinal feature of secondary development is the invention of new social devices that are intended to permit the society to adapt better . . . to the international situation."[2] There is a basic identification of development with innovation, and the prime mover of innovation has become the government, with obvious consequences for the role of the bureaucracy in society.

McClelland[3] and Hagen[4] have dealt more with the circumstances that seem to have produced individuals who are positively oriented towards innovation and, presumably, who would therefore be instrumental in the development process. McClelland ultimately decides that a compulsion to achieve is basic to an ability to innovate. Unfortunately, his indicators of this need to achieve for a society (children's stories) and of the conditions that promote its growth (the absence of men from the home and/or mass ideological changes) are not particularly relevant to the focus of the present study. Hagen's thesis, that a downward shift in the status of an elite group causes the members of the group to innovate in order to regain their previous status, is complementary to McClelland's, but equally irrelevant to Venezuela and most of Latin America. With the exception of Cuba no such deprivation has occurred.

Daniel Lerner[5] develops the simpler and more traditional theory that modern man develops in urban environments. The crucial event in this process is the move from the country to the city. Once in the city literacy is a necessity, and its acquisition triggers an increasing and reciprocal involvement with the mass media. This involvement in its turn leads to political participation, the phenomena most basic to Lerner's concept of a "modern" society.

What all these analyses have in common is their agreement that basic societal change is a constant companion of development. Whether it is cause or consequence is still debated. Certainly in Venezuela change, initiated by the impact of technology and products of the industrialized nations, is endemic. Adams's thesis that the governments of developing countries are engaging in social engineering is applicable to Venezuela. Under these conditions the public administration is a natural focus for the study of the effects of attitudes upon the implementation of policy.

Beginning with such a focus Riggs has developed the theory of prismatic society, a global model that provides a comprehensive framework for the analysis of administration in any country. His focus, however, is upon public administration in what he terms "transitional" societies: those nations in which the government has explicitly adopted a policy of change and development.[6] He finds that "modernization . . . may refer not to a particular kind of change, like 'industrialization,' but Westernization, or Hellenization, but to a phenomenon of historical relativity, to the processes which result whenever a society or state launches willingly—or unwillingly—a chain of transformations designed to reduce the cultural, religious, military, or technological gap between itself and some other society or state which it admires as more powerful, advanced, or prestigious."[7] The aim of innovation in a transitional society is thus relative to the model and pressures seen by the innovators.

Of special interest to us is Riggs's analysis of authority and control within the public administration and his concept of polynormativism. Beginning with the observed phenomenon of highly centralized bureaucracies in most transitional societies, he draws a distinction between authority—the right to make decisions—and control—the power to implement them.[8] His point is that these two factors are usually located at two different levels in the bureaucracies of transitional societies. Authority is centralized at the top and control is dispersed at the bottom. Formal reorganizations, aimed at either increased centralization or increased decentralization, fail to deal with this problem of a lack of integration of authority and control because such reorganization does not change the attitudes of those responsible for it. In this analysis the attitudes and values of the personnel involved are of crucial importance to any reform designed to reintegrate authority and control, since they are in large part responsible for it. This is so because individuals in prismatic societies, according to Riggs, hold conflicting norms, only one of which might be described as Weberian. In any particular case, this value is very likely to be overridden by other, more immediate, values.

Such a situation is described by Riggs as "polynormative." While holding for all societies, this condition is considered to be particularly acute in transitional nations. Here old and new norms are frequently and obviously in conflict and it is often difficult for individuals to determine a proper basis for decisions.

The application to our research is clear. Individuals are neither unidimensional nor able to completely separate the norms associated with differing roles in society. Therefore, it is unrealistic to assume that attitudes applicable to administrative situations will be entirely consistent with any one value structure. Moreover, a Riggsian analysis of bureaucracy focuses attention upon authority relations as the key variables within administrative settings. We have already discussed these factors in the context of administrative reform. Our survey, in its investigation of attitudes towards innovation especially, concentrates upon the respondent's attitudes towards authority. An effort is also made to determine the strength of perceived family ties and relate them to the administrative values held by the respondent. While it is expected that the respondents will prove to be polynormative (that is, their family and authority norms will tend to contradict their efficiency norms), a major goal of the research will be to determine the effect this polynormativism has upon the choices of the respondent when confronted with items that place family and administrative values in conflict. It should be noted, finally, that the concept of prismatic society embraces all polities. That is, societies are differentiated by the degree and kind of polynormativism they possess rather than by the presence or absence of quality.

One clear advantage of the prismatic model is that because its elements are based upon familiar patterns of research, work done within its framework is comparable to previous research. Riggs is basically a structural/functionalist and a Parsonian, and as such is in the mainstream of contemporary political theory. The present study uses prismatic theory for its global framework but in intent and method can be traced directly to Morroe Berger's seminal study of Egyptian bureaucrats.[9] Berger concentrated upon the "westernization" of the respondents in terms of their attitudes towards (among others) rationality, efficiency, hierarchy, and discretion. Perhaps because the equation of "westernization" and "modernization" was not made explicit but more probably because the design of the study did not allow for the "nonwestern" conditions under which the "westernized" bureaucrats lived and worked, the results were inconclusive.

Subsequent studies have become more aware of the consequences of this kind of confusion and, one hopes, more able to make the necessary distinctions. Daland and Motta's study of high level Brazilian bureaucrats is basically an adaptation of Berger's, using the prismatic model for global theory.[10] The present work is a replication of Daland and Motta with variables for family ties, polynormative choice, and family background added. As such, of course, it is comparable with both of the earlier works. It is also comparable in its background data with Hopkins's study of Peruvian bureaucrats[11] and with Warner's study of United States executives,[12] upon which Hopkins's work is based. The attitudes expressed by our respondents will be marginally comparable with those described by Weaver in his study of Guatemalan administrators.[13]

All of the above works assume that attitudes are relevant to behavior, and behavior relevant to structure and procedures. Even granted that these assumptions are valid, however, a difficulty remains. Innovation is a basic part of the concept of development, modernization, or whatever term is used to denote progressive or even nonprogressive societal change. It may be argued that efficiency is an irrelevant criterion in situations which frequently involve crises and almost always involve rapidly changing societal factors. One simple answer is that developing nations, including Venezuela, simply cannot afford the consequences of massive governmental inefficiency.

Such an objection to efficiency criteria can also be met on other grounds. The basic objection is not to efficiency as such but to the way in which the classical Weberian ideal defines it. If efficiency is defined as the ability to produce the greatest possible output from the fewest possible resources in terms of manifest policy implementation, then efficiency is clearly applicable to development administration. The rationale to this objection is that administrative efficiency demands order, regularity, and predictability as well as rigorous accounting and fiscal responsibility. These characteristics are held to be incompatible with the innovation necessary to cope effectively with the fluid situations engendered by societal change. That is, administrative efficiency is attacked on the grounds that its output is inadequate to deal with the problems a changing society faces. Efficiency may be fine for a government oriented towards the status quo, but it is an inappropriate criterion for one interested in changing the status quo or attempting to direct and manage change.

It is apparent that this objection is itself based upon efficiency criteria. If policies cannot be implemented by a bureaucracy in such a way that they deal effectively with the problems they were designed to solve, then they cannot be termed efficient. The problem here is one of scope. The criteria of efficiency in any particular case depend upon the goals involved. The objection accepts the Weberian definition of bureaucracy as a system that holds innovation by administrators to a minimum in the interests of "efficiency." The logical extension is that this sort of efficiency is unsuited to countries undergoing substantial changes. That is, a much more adaptable bureaucracy is needed to administer policies dealing with fluid situations. The situation is, in effect, the reverse of that which occasioned the Prussian bureaucracy that Weber took as his model. The situation then was one of widespread anarchy and disorder resulting from the religious wars of the seventeenth century. The Prussian bureaucracy that was created to cope with this situation not only sought to impose a stable and unchanging status quo but recruited its members, especially in its lower ranks, from the army, where socialization in the new norms had been particularly thorough.

The situation facing Venezuela is of the opposite sort. In this case, the bureaucracy is staffed with personnel who reflect the multiplicity of values existing in society and are themselves a part of the fluid situation. As Riggs has theorized and as we have described the Venezuelan bureaucracy, increased rigidity within the bureaucracy leads to the concentration of authority and control at opposite ends of the hierarchy, and as such is counterproductive in terms of overall governmental efficiency. If the Weberian model is not accepted as suitable, the objections to efficiency as a relevant criterion of development administration appear to be inappropriate, for they are based upon the ideal Weberian model that posits administrative rigidity as a prerequisite for efficiency. The crux of the objection is that efficiency and innovation cannot coexist within a bureaucracy. One of the major purposes of this study is to discover whether or not our respondents agree with such a dichotomy.

VI.

EFFICIENCY

Efficiency, defined as the ability to produce the greatest possible output from the fewest possible resources in terms of manifest policy implementation, is one of the primary concerns of administrative reform in Venezuela. The Venezuelan government is acutely aware of the limited nature of oil revenues and of the practically unlimited need for governmental funds in the development of the nation. Moreover, politics in Venezuela are now stable and regularized. It is only natural that an increased emphasis upon governmental efficiency should result.

While a general measure of the efficiency of policy implementation is difficult to construct because of the differing conditions and goals of each particular case, it is possible to construct a series of questions that measure an individual's attitudes towards efficiency. Using Daland and Motta's questions as a base, twelve items (Table 1) were constructed around the common theme of bureaucratic efficiency. The respondents are almost unanimous in rejecting the idea that personal trust and loyalty should take precedence over efficiency (item 1). That efficiency itself is the only meaningful criterion in administration, on the other hand, is rejected by most of the respondents; only 37 percent disagree with the idea that efficiency can be overemphasized (item 12). It is interesting that this question created the largest number of nonresponses (13, about 8 percent). Most probably the high nonresponse rate was a result of conflicting criteria and a bias towards efficiency that at least kept these respondents from agreeing with what is logically a rather reasonable statement. What is perhaps more interesting is that only half the respondents felt that the completion of tasks assigned to the public servant ought to be the most important criterion for evaluating him (item 11). The requirement that public servants finish the work assigned them would seem to be a minimal requirement for the efficient functioning of any organization. Moreover, only 57 percent felt that inefficient public servants should be removed from the public service (item 10), since it is fairly certain that being fired would cause personal problems for the person discharged.

TABLE 1. Efficiency Items

		%	Percentage agreeing with efficiency value
1. It would be useful in improving administration to promote only persons in whom one has confidence, even if they are not very efficient.	not useful at all not very useful useful very useful	59 39 1 1	98 (NR = 1)
2. It would be useful in improving governmental administration to establish an effective system of equal pay for work of equal difficulty and responsibility in all governmental positions.	very useful useful not very useful not useful at all	55 39 5 1	94 (NR = 1)
3. In general it is not advisable to show superior ability in administration; this could cause jealousy and provoke hostility.	completely disagree disagree agree completely agree	44 48 4 4	92 (NR = 1)
4. In order to maintain a climate of reasonable tranquility in administration, it is desirable not to insist that everyone work energetically.	completely disagree disagree agree completely agree	26 61 9 3	87 (NR = 2)
5. Appointment of public servants should be based only on the ability and talent of the candidates.	completely agree agree disagree completely disagree	35 46 17 1	81 (NR = 1)
6. It would be useful in improving governmental administration to increase the standards necessary for admission to the public service.	very useful useful not very useful not useful at all	28 53 16 1	81 (NR = 4)

TABLE 1. *continued*

		Percent	Percentage agreeing with efficiency value
7. If the public service doesn't value people who render work of high quality, it is better for those people to limit themselves to the satisfaction of the minimum requirements of their jobs.	completely disagree disagree agree completely agree	30 45 18 5	75 (NR = 4)
8. Public servants who work more ought to be paid more.	completely agree agree disagree completely disagree	27 36 29 4	63 (NR = 6)
9. Capacity for producing work should always be the most important factor in the promotion of public servants.	completely agree agree disagree completely disagree	15 46 32 5	61 (NR = 3)
10. Inefficient civil servants ought not to be removed from the public service if this creates some personal problems for the removed.	completely disagree disagree agree completely agree	7 50 28 14	57 (NR = 2)
11. The most important standard for evaluating the quality of a public servant is whether he executes tasks confided him.	completely agree agree disagree completely disagree	8 43 44 4	51 (NR = 2)
12. Some people overemphasize the idea of efficiency in administration to the prejudice of other values.	completely disagree disagree agree completely agree	3 34 41 14	37 (NR = 13)

Note: Total N equals 153. The percentages given do not exclude the nonresponses. In the last item, for example, nonresponses account for 8 percent of the respondents. They have not been excluded because they are of interest in themselves in that they aid our understanding of the impact of the question upon the respondents, especially when they are numerous. Because of their inclusion the percentages given do not usually sum to 100. Where they do it is because of rounding, since all the items had at least one nonresponse.

The general picture emerging from the responses to these questions is that of a strong acceptance of efficiency values and a personal willingness to put them into practice (items 3, 4, and 7) coupled with a much less strong desire to see them implemented on a general basis (items 9 through 11). This seems to be based upon a regard for personnel already within the system rather than a more generalized concern (items 5 and 6), especially when it comes to evaluation and promotion (items 9 and 11). The general feeling seems to be a strong but not overwhelming concern with efficiency that becomes weakest when the implementation of efficiency norms would adversely effect the careers of other individuals.

An efficiency index has been so constructed that a score of 100 would indicate that the individual "completely agreed" (or "completely disagreed" if the item was negatively phrased) with all the statements concerning efficiency, while a score of −100 would indicate complete disagreement with these items. Someone who simply "agreed" or "disagreed" with all the items would have a score of +50 or −50, while a person who was evenly balanced between the two types of responses would have a score of 0. A nonresponse was deleted from the individual's index and had no effect upon his score. The highest score recorded was +83 and the lowest −17. The scores averaged 36 and the standard deviation was 19. That is, the scores are rather widely distributed between the highest and lowest scores achieved. The distribution is skewed slightly (0.145) towards the lower end of the scale, but for all practical purposes we have a wide normal distribution over the 100 points between the highest and lowest scores.

Perhaps the most obvious factor that could influence efficiency scores is the job placement of the individual respondent. It is reasonable to suppose that those most concerned with efficiency would be those who have the most to gain (or lose) from the efficiency of others. Table 2 tends to support this hypothesis. If the type of job held by the respondent is further divided by distinguishing between line and staff positions the picture becomes more interesting (Table 3). Line chiefs are slightly more concerned with efficiency than their staff counterparts and middle level executives are equal in their concern, but respondents who are responsible for only their own efficiency are quite different. While staff noncommand respondents are as concerned with efficiency as their immediate

TABLE 2. Efficiency Scores by Job Level

	Department Heads	Division or Section Heads	Noncommand Personnel
Average Efficiency Score	43 (16)	36 (80)	34 (57)

Note: The numbers in parentheses represent the number of respondents in each category.

TABLE 3. Efficiency Scores by Job Level and Type

	Department Heads	Division or Section Heads	Noncommand Personnel
Line	45 (9)	36 (41)	30 (18)
Staff	42 (7)	36 (39)	36 (39)

superiors, line personnel at this level seem to be less concerned with this value than of the other groups.

It may be, however, that the type of job held by the respondent is less important than his age. One might argue that a younger respondent would be more likely to emphasize efficiency because of its importance to national development, while older administrators would be more likely to temper this criterion with a deeper sympathy for human values. The data did not support this hypothesis, there being no significant differences by age. The same results were found when efficiency scores were computed by time served in the public service.

Job levels and types remain the strongest predictors of efficiency concerns. On an overall basis the relation between age and efficiency scores is .07 (Pearson's r), which means that they are not related. The relation between time in the public service and a respondent's efficiency score is equally weak (.06).

Younger respondents who have attained command positions

do seem to have a greater concern with efficiency than the average respondent. The 27 respondents who were thirty years old or younger and had attained the position of division or section chief averaged 39 on the efficiency index, three points higher than the average for that job group. The same age group in noncommand positions (30 persons) averaged 32, two points below the average for their job level. The differences are not particularly great but they do suggest that a concern for efficiency may have been a factor in the early promotions.

It is possible, however, that differences of sex are skewing these patterns. One might suppose that women, especially Latin American women, would be more positively oriented towards human considerations than men and because of this would have lower efficiency scores. The opposite is true. Dividing the respondents by sex reveals that men averaged 35 points on the efficiency index but women averaged 40. Women formed 26 percent of the sample and, with two exceptions, occupied staff and line jobs in about the same proportions as men. Women are overrepresented in noncommand staff jobs (45 percent of the women vs. 19 percent of the men) and underrepresented in intermediate command line jobs (10 percent of the women vs. 33 percent of the men). If we compare the efficiency levels of men and women in staff noncommand positions we find that male staff analysts tend to be high or low, but most of them are low. Most female staff analysts have high efficiency orientations and only one out of five has a low orientation. In sum, women are more positively oriented towards efficiency than men, and in the one case where there were enough women to make generalization possible, this difference was stronger than the difference by job level. Nevertheless, the original patterns found by job level for men were not generally changed, although male staff analysts were found to be somewhat less concerned with efficiency than their line counterparts, a reversal of the situation found with the full sample. It is clear that the earlier finding was heavily influenced by the overrepresentation of women in this category. On the other hand, job level remains the strongest indicator of efficiency concerns, holding for both men and women. The higher the job level, the higher the average concern with efficiency.

A division by the type of organization (80 ministerial personnel vs. 73 nonministerial) in which respondents worked was found to have little effect upon efficiency scores.

A comparison of efficiency responses by job location was made, partly because of the frequently encountered feeling in Venezuela that Caracas is qualitatively different in its culture from the interior. A more specific hypothesis in an administrative context is that the negative effects of the extreme centralization of public agencies in Venezuela will be more acute in the interior than in the capital, where agency headquarters are located. If, as has been argued, authority relations are generally personalized as well as highly centralized, it follows that they will be less efficient where face-to-face contact is not possible. This is the case with those administrators in the interior, for unless they go to Caracas they are forced to rely primarily upon the telephone or the mails. The situation is exacerbated by the rather slow Venezuelan mail services. In the capital this is overcome through the use of messengers, a device both expensive and time consuming for interior personnel.

The result is increased delay leading, presumably, to increased frustration with the system for those of our respondents who work in the interior. Moreover, the assumed cultural differences between Caracas and the interior might lead to further misunderstandings between Caracas and interior personnel. It would be surprising if the result of these factors was not an increased concern with efficiency in the interior.

The 39 respondents located in the interior did in fact average higher efficiency scores than the 114 in Caracas (42 vs. 34), a result made even more significant by the fact that 90 percent of the female respondents work in Caracas. When further divided by sex these differences are highly visible (Table 4). Respondents who work in the interior are more concerned with efficiency than those who work in Caracas whether they are men or women, but women retain their higher average scores across all groups.

TABLE 4. Average Efficiency Scores by Job Location and Sex

	Caracas	Interior
Men	32	40
	(78)	(35)
Women	38	55
	(36)	(4)

If location of office is crossed with job levels and average efficiency scores, the same pattern emerges. Job levels and types remain a strong indicator of efficiency scores, but in all but one case (staff department heads) efficiency scores for respondents working in the interior are significantly higher than those of their counterparts in Caracas.

A further investigation of this theme leads us to nonbureaucratic variables such as the environment in which the respondents grew up. Following Lerner's theory, respondents who spent their infancy and adolesence in urban environments should be more "modern" than those from a rural environment. Our data tends to confirm this thesis (Table 5). The differences are not greatly pronounced. Since Lerner's thesis is not that modernization leads to urbanization, but rather the reverse, "urban" has been defined here as all the state capitals, Caracas, and the remaining major industrial or commercial centers of Venezuela.

TABLE 5. Efficiency Averages by Infant and Adolescent Environment of Respondents

	Urban	Rural, Small Town and Rural/ Small Town	Rural/Urban and Small Town/ Urban
Efficiency	37	32	37
Averages	(116)	(21)	(16)

More specific geographic divisions are also of interest in the Venezuelan case. Two areas in Venezuela are thought by Venezuelans to be significantly different from the rest of the country. The first is Caracas, which has already been discussed. The second is the Venezuelan Andes, consisting of the states of Táchira, Médira, and Trujillo. The people of the Andes (Andinos) are traditionally considered serious, hard working, religious, and strongly familial. In our case these traditional attributes might be reflected in a heightened concern for efficiency. A further assumption along this line is that a foreign upbringing might result in attitudes different from those of the native Venezuelans (Table 6).

The direction of these assumptions appears to be correct, but

[60] *Change and Bureaucracy*

TABLE 6. Efficiency Averages by Place of Respondent's
Infancy and Adolescence

	Caracas	Andes	Other Venezuela	Foreign	Caracas/ Andes	Caracas/ Other Venezuela	Caracas/ Foreign
Efficiency	38	38	35	41	42	28	46
Average	(58)	(17)	(41)	(7)	(5)	(24)	(1)

there is one aspect of the table that is puzzling. Both Caraqueños
and Andinos score slightly higher than the average respondent on
the efficiency index, while foreigners score even higher. The differences for Venezuelans are not great but they are in the predicted
direction. Being brought up in a foreign country, Caracas and the
Andes, or Caracas and a foreign country seems to result in higher
concerns with efficiency, but the number of respondents who have
experienced these conditions is too small for these results to be
conclusive. What is more puzzling is the marked drop in efficiency
scores for those raised in both Caracas and non-Andean parts of
Venezuela. No other group is as low in efficiency scores as this
one, and there are enough respondents in it to render it significant.
One possible explanation is that these respondents had neither the
foreign background nor the strong Andean family ties to cushion
the shock of living in Caracas, and that their reaction has been to
become relatively indifferent to such values as efficiency. This is
purely speculation, however, for there is nothing in our data to
explain this result.

If the same variables are applied to the respondents' fathers a
quite different picture emerges (Table 7). The reasoning here is that
the marked mobility revealed in Table 6 (it will be remembered that
114 of the respondents are presently working in Caracas, while
only 58 were raised there) might have resulted in situations in
which family traditions are more important than the regional traditions of the place in which the respondent was brought up.
Family mobility during the respondents' fathers' infancy and adolesence was in fact much less than for their sons and daughters,
only four of the fathers having mixed backgrounds as opposed to
thirty of their children. Unfortunately, the low number involved
does not permit generalizations from this group.

TABLE 7. Efficiency Averages by Place of Fathers'
Infancy and Adolescence

	Caracas	Andes	Other Venezuela	Foreign	Caracas/ Andes	Caracas/ Other Venezuela	Caracas/ Foreign
Efficiency	27	38	37	37	—	35	33
Averages	(19)	(29)	(79)	(21)	(0)	(2)	(2)

NR = 1

Those groups that are relatively numerous are all within four points of the previous groups (Table 6) except for those whose fathers grew up in Caracas. These respondents averaged only 27 points on the efficiency index compared to the 38 points averaged by all those growing up in Caracas. A possible explanation for this difference is that Caracas was a very different city before 1939 (the average date of birth of the respondents) than it became afterwards. The reasoning here is that these respondents grew up in Caracas in families that were themselves native to the city, and thus did not experience the culture shock experienced by most of the others. This hypothesis would, of course, find the cause of attitude change more in geographical mobility and change than in the nature of urban life itself. Such a supposition would be contrary to Lerner's thesis that an urban environment by itself induces "modernity" in its inhabitants.

Social mobility as well as geographical mobility might have a causative influence upon attitude change. Hagen in particular has advanced this thesis, arguing that the status deprivation engendered by downward social mobility is important. For this reason we have analyzed the social class of our respondents and their fathers. Class rankings were determined by the perceptions of the respondents.

Not surprisingly, the majority of our respondents saw themselves as middle class, although a substantial number perceived themselves as upper middle class (Table 8). There is a tendency for those who see themselves as upper middle class to have higher efficiency scores, but the difference is not great. Those who see themselves as lower middle class have significantly lower scores but are not sufficiently numerous to justify generalization.

TABLE 8. Efficiency Averages by Respondents' Social Class

	Upper	Upper Middle	Middle	Lower Middle	Lower
Efficiency	29	39	36	25	42
Averages	(1)	(39)	(106)	(6)	(1)

Hagen's thesis deals with formerly upper class groups that have lost a highly privileged position. A somewhat broadened version would posit that any downward class movement would result in a strong desire to regain the lost social position. On the general assumption that class mobility will have more effect upon attitudes than present class, the respondents were divided according to their perceptions of their father's class (Table 9) and then according to the relations between the respondent's class and his father's class (Table 10).

TABLE 9. Efficiency Averages by Social Class of Respondent's Father

	Upper	Upper Middle	Middle	Lower Middle	Lower
Efficiency	33	38	36	33	41
Averages	(1)	(22)	(78)	(41)	(11)

The same pattern of lower efficiency scores accompanying lower class rankings is repeated, but this is again true only within the middle class. There are not enough respondents with upper class fathers to warrant discussion (as a point of interest, the individual who ranked himself as upper class had an upper middle class father; the upper class father noted here has an upper middle class son). There is, however, a fair sized number of respondents (11) who report having lower class fathers. Since even the one individual who reported himself as lower class is, by accepted standards in Venezuela, at least lower middle class (i.e., he wears a coat and tie and has an office job with the government), all these respondents are reporting themselves as upwardly mobile. The figures in

TABLE 10. Efficiency Averages by Relation between Respondent's and Respondent's Father's Social Class

	Respondent Higher than Father	Respondent Same as Father	Respondent Lower than Father
Efficiency Average	37 (67)	35 (78)	31 (8)

Table 10 tend to contradict Hagen's thesis that status deprivation results in more "modern" views, if it is broadened to include any class movement. Upward rather than downward mobility seems to result in higher efficiency scores. It may be argued, on the other hand, (1) that Hagen was interested more in innovation than in efficiency, and (2) that movement within the middle class, which is primarily what is represented here, is relatively insignificant for his thesis. Since there is only one respondent reporting an upper class father when he himself is of a lower class, and there are no respondents reporting a middle class father when the respondent perceives himself to be lower class (the respondent who reported himself as lower class also reported having a lower class father), there have been no major downward movements among the respondents. Still, the perception that there has been downward mobility in their lives is reported by eight respondents, and they have a slightly lower efficiency score than other groups. The implication is that at least one "modern" value is negatively rather than positively affected by status deprivation.

Correspondingly, a move from the lower class to the middle class has higher efficiency scores associated with it than any other group. Again, this would tend to contradict Hagen's thesis for at least this one value. It would, however, support the more general thesis that class mobility leads to more "modern" values.

Our final nonbureaucratic variable is graduate training. An undergraduate degree is a general requirement for entry into ENAP's graduate courses, and all but five respondents held such a degree. Of those who did, 29 had received graduate training other than ENAP's. There is a strong indication (Table 11) that graduate training is associated with increased concern for efficiency, those respondents with graduate experience previous to their enrollment

TABLE 11. Efficiency Averages by Location of Respondent's
Graduate Schools (other than ENAP)

	No Graduate School	Venezuelan Graduate Schools	European and North American Graduate Schools	Latin American Graduate Schools
Efficiency	35	37	45	40
Average	(123)	(18)	(9)	(2)
				NR = 1

in ENAP averaging 40 points on the efficiency index, some five points higher than their colleagues who had no such training. It is a moot point, however, whether the graduate training increased concern for efficiency or whether these respondents were selected (or self-selected) for graduate training because of their positive attitudes towards "modern" values. Since European and North American schools generally carry the most prestige in Venezuela, the second explanation would account for the higher scores achieved by the respondents who attended these institutions, quite apart from any effect the schools had upon their values. At any rate, graduate training does not have a negative effect upon efficiency concerns and in the case of both foreign and domestic schools is associated with increased concern for this value.

In sum, efficiency scores are strongly affected by job levels, sex, job location, major upward class mobility, and foreign graduate training. They are somewhat less affected by job type, location of infancy and adolesence, and domestic graduate training. Efficiency scores are very little or not at all affected by age, time in the public service, or ministerial/nonministerial status.

The only factor linking all the variables that have a major effect upon efficiency scores, with the possible exception of job location, is change. Promotion, for example, can be seen as a major change for the individual involved, as can major upward class mobility and foreign graduate training. That women average higher scores than men can also be seen as the result of a change in status when it is remembered that the inclusion of women in Venezuelan public service as executives is a very recent development.

Whether or not the location of a job in the interior is a change depends, of course, upon whether or not the individual concerned grew up there. An analysis of efficiency scores by job locations and native regions reveals that in every case those working in the interior have higher scores. Those raised in Caracas and working there (51) average 37, which is slightly above average, but those raised in Caracas and working in the interior (7) average 44. This might be taken as support for the theory that major change of almost any sort results in increased efficiency scores were it not for the fact that those respondents both raised and working in the interior (20) also average 44, while those raised in the interior and working in Caracas (38) average 32. Those native to foreign countries averaged 36 when working in Caracas (5) and 52 when working in the interior (2). The positive effect of working in the interior is quite independent of the native regions of the respondents. This is also true of those with mixed backgrounds. These respondents averaged 29 when working in Caracas (22) and 34 when working in the interior (10).

Our earliest explanation for these differences, based upon the assumption that working conditions differ, would seem to be more valid for this variable than one based upon a general theory of change. Nevertheless, change does seem to have strong explanatory power for most of the variables associated with major differences in efficiency scores. Because of this the following section on innovation will pursue the general subject of change, primarily through an innovation index. A major possibility is that changes in attitudes towards authority relations (the basic component of the innovation items) will tend to be associated with other changes in the respondent's bureaucratic and personal life.

VII.

INNOVATION

In a country changing as much and as rapidly as Venezuela, innovation, defined here as changes in the way things are done, is not only necessary but in the long run inevitable. The need for innovation within the public bureaucracy may be as great as in society as a whole, but there does not seem to be any particular hastening towards the inevitable within governmental organizations. On the national level the Venezuelan government since the 1930s has been change-oriented, if the appearance of new and different agencies can be regarded as change. Nonministerial organizations of all sizes and shapes have been created in diverse fields of activity and new organizations continue to appear.

The diversity shown in the creation of organizations, however, has not been matched by innovations in their internal organization. Hierarchical structures with dispersed responsibility but highly concentrated authority are the rule. With very few exceptions all authority is located at the top of an organization and in Caracas. The problems discussed in the previous sections have made innovation in authority relations and structures a natural focus for administrative reform.

While attempts have been made to disperse agencies throughout the country, almost all governmental agencies retain their headquarters and very nearly all their decision-making prerogatives in Caracas. Few if any organizations have dispersed internal decision-making power. Delays in implementation are common as line personnel request authority to deal with new situations and agency heads struggle with the large number of decisions that they alone can make.

Before considering attitudes towards the dispersal of decision making power, however, we will first examine the respondents' attitudes towards innovation itself and compare these with their attitudes towards efficiency.

Table 12 contains the questions focused upon innovation. Compared with the items on efficiency, two aspects are noteworthy: first, that the respondents are more favorably inclined towards efficiency than towards innovation in administration; and second, that they are less positive in their responses to innovation items. Only item 3 attained over 26 percent responses in a "completely" agree or disagree category, while seven items on the efficiency scale attained or surpassed this level. Despite this relative lack of enthusiasm either for or against innovation, there are some clear patterns to the respondents' opinions. They are not hostile to innovation nor do they think it is necessarily harmful to administration or that administration is hostile to innovation (items 1 and 2). Moreover, they largely agree that higher bureaucratic positions should be occupied by individuals chosen primarily for their ability to innovate new solutions to problems (item 3).

They do not, however, feel that innovation should come at the expense of hierarchy, or that it is the primary virtue in administration. They reject by a large majority (65 percent) the proposition that a person without administrative experience or instruction in bureaucratic procedures can do anything except create difficulties (item 9) or that administrators should not strictly follow rules and regulations (item 8). They agree in almost the same degree (60 percent) that the strength of administration lies in the stability, order, and regularity of its processes (item 7). Consequently, it is hardly surprising that the respondents also agree (56 percent) that one of the most serious administrative problems is to maintain control over the work of subordinates (item 6).

What emerges from the items considered above is an acceptance of innovation as long as it does not seriously disturb existing administrative procedures. Since these procedures are, in the Venezuelan case, almost certainly centralized and authoritarian, it is difficult to see just how innovation on any but the highest levels could occur. Perhaps this distinction could explain the simultaneous agreement of 66 percent of the respondents to items 4 and 8. The first states that it is all right to break regulations if this facilitates the achievement of program goals; the second that it is usually bad for administration if bureaucrats do not strictly execute the written norms and rules. Not too surprisingly, the respondents were about evenly split on the idea that it is best to rely on methods already proven by experience in order to resolve administrative problems (item 5), although there was a slightly greater tendency to disagree than to agree.

The same explanation that suggested itself in the analysis of

TABLE 12. Innovation Items

		%	Percentage agreeing with innovation value
1. "Developmentalists" in the public service do more harm than good in aiding economic progress.	completely disagree	26	89
	disagree	63	
	agree	7	
	completely agree	1 (NR = 4)	
2. It is necessary to learn from the start that administrative work does not tolerate individuals who always want to introduce new ideas.	completely disagree	26	87
	disagree	61	
	agree	8	
	completely agree	3 (NR = 2)	
3. The most important standard for naming administrative heads and directors should be the capacity of individuals to find new solutions to problems.	completely agree	34	84
	agree	50	
	disagree	14	
	completely disagree	1 (NR = 2)	
4. It is all right to break regulations if this facilitates the achievement of program goals.	completely agree	11	66
	agree	55	
	disagree	26	
	completely disagree	6 (NR = 4)	
5. In order to resolve administrative problems it is best to rely on methods already proven by experience.	completely disagree	5	56
	disagree	51	
	agree	31	
	completely agree	13 (NR = 6)	
6. One of the most serious administrative problems is to maintain control over the work of subordinates.	completely disagree	6	44
	disagree	38	
	agree	43	
	completely agree	13 (NR = 0)	
7. A little innovation may be desirable, but the greatest strength of administration is found precisely in the stability, order, and regularity of its processes.	completely disagree	10	40
	disagree	30	
	agree	43	
	completely agree	12 (NR = 2)	

TABLE 12. *continued*

		%	Percentage agreeing with efficiency value
8. Sometimes administrators do not strictly execute the written norms and rules, and this is usually bad for administration.	completely disagree	5	34
	disagree	29	
	agree	46	
	completely agree	19 (NR = 2)	
9. Those who work in administration without previous authorization or instructions only create difficulties.	completely disagree	5	33
	disagree	28	
	agree	49	
	completely agree	16 (NR = 5)	

efficiency items seems to be applicable here: innovation criteria are attractive when applied by the individual to himself but are less attractive when applied to others—in this case, to subordinates. While this explanation is itself attractive, it does not agree very well with the distribution of innovation scores among respondents.

The innovation index was derived from the responses to the items focused on innovation in the same way the efficiency index was derived from the efficiency items. The range of scores was 100 points (the same as the efficiency range) but scores were more dispersed (a standard deviation of 22 as opposed to 19), and the average score was much lower than on the efficiency index. The innovation mean was 14 (efficiency $\bar{X} = 36$) and the high and low scores were 61 and -39. A normal curve was obtained, skewness being only $-.06$.

The hypothesis that innovation scores would be lower in proportion to the number of subordinates under the respondent's control is contradicted by the mean scores for job levels (Table 13). Even if it is argued that the relatively low scores on the absolute scale indicate that the department chiefs are primarily concerned with their own prerogatives rather than their subordinates' opportunities for initiating actions, the even lower scores of the noncommand respondents indicate that these respondents largely reject

TABLE 13. Innovation Averages by Job Levels

	Department Heads	Division or Section Heads	Nonchiefs
Innovation	24	13	12
Averages	(16)	(80)	(39)

innovation for themselves. While the scores are lower than those for efficiency items, the pattern is identical. The only major difference is that department heads are even farther apart from the other command levels on innovation scores than with efficiency scores. Innovation scores by job level and type (Table 14) again reveal the same pattern as the efficiency scores (Table 3). The line department heads are the most favorably oriented towards innovation and line noncommand respondents the least, with intermediate command in between but closer to the noncommand respondents. Once again staff noncommand respondents are about the same as their immediate supervisors. Staff department heads are higher than either group of intermediate command respondents but not as high as line department heads.

TABLE 14. Innovation Averages by Job Level and Type

	Department Heads	Divison or Section Heads	Nonchiefs
Line	26	14	8
	(9)	(41)	(18)
Staff	22	12	13
	(7)	(39)	(39)

A breakdown of average scores by age groups indicates that there is no particular correlation of innovation scores with age. On an overall basis, innovation correlates with age at a .29 level (Pearson's r). This indicates a slight positive relation between age and innovation scores as opposed to no relation at all between efficiency and age.

Younger respondents who have attained intermediate command positions have a tendency to be more positively oriented towards innovation values than their command level as a whole. The 27 respondents who were thirty years old or younger and had attained the position of division or section chief averaged 19 as opposed to 13 for all division and section chiefs. The same age group in noncommand positions averaged 10. On the other hand, the 9 respondents twenty-eight to thirty years old in staff noncommand positions averaged 21, so this age group is anything but consistent. Even so, the consistently high scores for young intermediate command respondents suggest that their positive concern for innovation may have been a factor in their early promotion, just as their higher average concern for efficiency may have been.

If innovation scores are divided by time in the public service a clearer picture emerges (Table 15). While the pattern is more consistent, the differences are not as great as those observed among job levels. It does indicate that concern for innovation rises with increased time in the public service for about ten years and then falls off, ultimately to a level lower than that for any other group. That the relation is not linear is confirmed by the low correlation of time in the public service with innovation scores ($r = .15$). Perhaps the most interesting aspect of the data here is that while efficiency concerns tend to increase with time in the public service, concern with innovation follows a quite different and more complex pattern.

These results may be skewed by sex, however. In our examination of efficiency criteria it was found that women were markedly more concerned with efficiency than men, especially at the staff noncommand level. On a straight division by sex, women also tend to be more positively oriented towards innovation than men (17 vs. 12). If innovation averages are broken down by job level and type and by sex, on the other hand, job levels and types are

TABLE 15. Innovation Averages by Time in the Public Service

14 or More Years	10–13	6–9	3–5	Less than 3
7	14	20	14	13
(29)	(34)	(32)	(34)	(24)

better overall predictors of innovation scores than sex. Women
have much lower scores in three categories, much higher scores in
two more, and are about equal with men in the third. There does
not seem to be any particular pattern involved. In general, divisions by sex of innovation scores simply emphasize the more powerful predictive value of job levels, even though women as a group
are more positively oriented towards innovation than men.

When job levels and types are divided by time in the public
service an interesting pattern emerges. Disregarding department
heads, where there are very few respondents with fewer than 10
years in the public service, there is a very strong tendency to begin
a career with a moderately positive orientation towards innovation, to become more and more in favor of innovation for the next
ten years, and then to become less positive as time goes on. Only
line department heads seem to retain their positive orientation
towards innovation as their experience accumulates, although promotion seems to have postponed the decline in interest for both
line and staff department heads. It may be that promotion is the
key to keeping a positive interest in innovation alive. At any rate,
positive innovation concerns on lower levels reach their peak six to
nine years after the respondent has entered the public service and
decline afterwards. Line department heads have exhibited no significant decline and staff department heads decline only after thirteen years of service, but the number of respondents involved at
these command levels is so small that no generalizations can be
made.

It was suggested earlier that respondents working in nonministerial agencies might be more positively oriented towards efficiency
because the legal status of their organizations is not as restrictive
as that of the more traditional ministries and because most of these
agencies are designed to serve specific developmental purposes. It
was found that both the efficiency score averages and levels were
slightly higher for nonministerial respondents than for their colleagues in the ministries. The same argument can be made for innovation concerns, but when innovation scores are computed the
reverse situation is found. The 80 ministerial respondents are more
positively oriented towards innovation ($\bar{X} = 16$) than the 73 nonministerial respondents ($\bar{X} = 12$). The difference is not great, but
its direction tends to refute the hypothesis that nonministerial respondents are more innovative than those working in the older

organizations. This, of course, supports the idea that the internal structure and conditions of work in the nonministerial agencies are traditional in nature.

Equally interesting is the finding that the 39 respondents working in the interior are not more favorably disposed towards innovation ($\bar{X} = 14$) than the 114 respondents working in Caracas ($\bar{X} = 14$). It will be recalled that respondents located in the interior were significantly higher in their efficiency concerns than those in Caracas. A logical response to the frustrating position in which we have assumed them to be would be a positive attitude towards innovation, since if they themselves had more authority their frustration with delays in communicating with Caracas would be lessened. They did not have higher innovation averages, although when respondents are further divided by sex there is a very slight tendency in this direction (men in the interior averaged 14 and those in Caracas 12). Since 90 percent of the female respondents are located in Caracas and since as a group they tend towards higher innovation scores, it is not surprising that their deletion from the table affects the scores of the Caracas respondents.

If the average innovation score for these categories is further divided by job location, however, those in command positions in the interior are in all but one case much more favorable towards innovation than their Caracas counterparts. In the one instance where this does not occur (line division and section heads have a lower average score in the interior) there is only a 2-point difference. For the other three command groups interior respondents average 15 points higher than their Caracas colleagues.

The lowest average score was that of the interior noncommand respondents. Line respondents at this level, the group least in favor of innovation, are joined in the interior by their staff counterparts, a deviation from the usual pattern. It may be that subordinate personnel in general and those in the interior in particular do not wish to see their immediate superiors with more authority. This is consistent with prismatic theory, which would place control with this group and authority at the highest hierarchical level. A delegation of authority to lower levels would threaten this control.

Nonbureaucratic variables also have major impacts upon innovation scores. The degree of urbanization in our respondents' backgrounds (Table 16) strongly affects innovation scores. Under Lerner's thesis, however, those raised entirely in an urban envir-

TABLE 16. Innovation Averages by Infant and Adolescent
Environment of Respondent

	Urban	Rural, Small Town and Rural/ Small Town	Rural/Urban and Small Town/ Urban
Innovation	14	8	21
Averages	(116)	(21)	(16)

onment should have the highest scores, those raised in both urban
and rural environments medium scores, and those who have grown
up entirely in nonurban environments the lowest scores. The entirely rural group does in fact have the lowest scores, but it is the
group that experienced both environments while growing up that
has the highest scores. The implication is that cultural change in
the environment has more of an effect upon innovation scores than
either urban or rural environments by themselves. Even so, the
data here tend to support the thesis that rural environments tend
to produce individuals less prone to innovation than urban environments.

When the respondents are divided by geographic regions (Table
17) a quite different pattern from that with efficiency scores is encountered. Respondents raised outside Venezuela in particular

TABLE 17. Innovation Averages by Place of Respondent's
Infancy and Adolesence

	Caracas	Andes	Other Venezuela	Foreign	Caracas/ Andes	Caracas/ Other Venezuela	Caracas/ Foreign
Innovation	18	11	12	1	12	14	0
Averages	(58)	(17)	(41)	(7)	(5)	(24)	(1)

show a divergent pattern. This group had the highest efficiency
rating of any geographic group, but it has by far the lowest innovation scores. It may be that a result of this particular combination

of environments leads more to an acceptance of authority patterns in the host country than to any challenge to them, but the number involved is too small to allow for much speculation. Of more interest to us is that Caraqueños have averaged higher innovation scores than any other regional group. A combination of Andean or other Venezuelan background and Caracas does not result in a marked difference from either background alone, again in contrast to efficiency scores. The averages for the mixed backgrounds are somewhat higher than for the nonmixed, however, and this coupled with the markedly higher scores for Caraqueños supports the thesis that Caracas is more innovative (or less traditional) than the interior. Moreover, there seems to be a direct relationship between a Caracas environment and higher innovation scores. Even so, the differences among scores are not great, although the direction is consistent.

A division of the respondents by their fathers' native regions (Table 18) results in innovation averages that are even closer together than those in which the native environment of the respon-

TABLE 18. Innovation Averages of Respondents by Father's Place of Infancy and Adolesence

	Caracas	Andes	Other Venezuela	Foreign	Caracas/ Andes	Caracas/ Other Venezuela	Caracas/ Foreign
Innovation	16	16	14	9	—	14	8
Averages	(19)	(29)	(79)	(21)	(0)	(2)	(2)

NR = 1

dents is considered. This might indicate that environmental factors are more important for innovation concerns than family traditions. The differences from Table 17 are not large but all change is towards the average score rather than away from it. It will be remembered that those respondents whose fathers were natives of Caracas were substantially lower on the efficiency index than any of the other groups, an anomaly in that respondents native to Caracas had above average efficiency scores. This is not the case with innovation scores. The answer may lie in social mobility rather than geographic mobility. In any case, Caracas does seem to influence those raised in it towards innovation, and there are no particularly negative effects upon innovation scores involved with being a member of a family in Caracas for two generations. Native Andinos have below average scores, but to be the child of an Andino does not seem to have a negative effect. A combination of urban and non-urban environments while growing up, however, is associated with the highest average innovation scores for all background factors examined so far.

Present social class does not affect innovation scores a great deal, although there is some evidence that those who identify themselves as lower middle class are as indifferent to innovation as they are to efficiency. A division by the respondents' fathers' class (Table 19) reveals a tendency for a drop in innovation scores as the fathers' class recedes from the middle class. Perhaps most interesting here

TABLE 19.   Innovation Averages by Respondents' Fathers' Social Class

	Upper	Upper Middle	Middle	Lower Middle	Lower
Innovation	22	14	15	12	10
Averages	(1)	(22)	(78)	(41)	(11)

is the low average score of those whose fathers were lower class. It will be remembered that this group had the highest efficiency scores of any class grouping, either of the respondents or of their fathers. It would appear that upward class mobility, at least from the lower class, does not lead to high average innovation scores. In fact, the reverse seems to occur.

A division by class mobility (Table 20) tends to support this hypothesis. Upward mobility or no mobility have no effect upon innovation scores, but downward mobility results in a high concern with innovation. The pattern is the opposite of that encountered with efficiency scores and is, of course, consistent with Hagen's thesis that status deprivation results in innovative behavior. Un-

TABLE 20. Innovation Averages by Relation between Respondents
and Respondents' Fathers' Scoial Class

	Respondent Higher than Father	*Respondent Same as Father*	*Respondent Lower than Father*
Innovation	13	13	21
Averages	(67)	(78)	(8)

fortunately, the number reporting downward mobility is not large
enough to allow for decisive generalization.

A division of the respondents by graduate training (Table 21)
also reveals patterns quite different from those found with efficiency scores. Those patterns indicated that efficiency scores rose

TABLE 21. Innovation Averages by Location of Respondent's
Graduate Schools

	No Graduate Schools	*Venezuelan Graduate Schools*	*European and North American Graduate Schools*	*Latin American Graduate Schools*
Innovation	14	10	21	39
Averages	(123)	(18)	(9)	(2)

NR = 1

in all cases of graduate training, with the most prestigious schools
associated with the highest scores. To some extent that pattern is
repeated here, for European, North American, and non-Venezuelan
Latin American schools are all associated with high innovation
scores. The very high scores of the last group are of particular
interest, but unfortunately the very small number of respondents
involved precludes speculation upon possible causes. The surprising development is the low innovation scores associated with
domestic graduate programs. The same group had moderately
high efficiency scores. It may be that authority relationships within
Venezuelan universities are much the same as those found in Vene-

zuelan public service, a hypothesis supported by our own experience. That is, they are much more oriented towards tradition and authority than change. The implication of this finding is clear if our analysis is correct: innovation is an attitude uncommon in Venezuelan graduate schools, and a special effort is called for if administrators are to be positively motivated towards this value by graduate schools.

On an overall basis a concern with innovation is positively and consistently related to job levels, status deprivation, and foreign graduate work. It is related on a nonlinear basis to time in the public service, job location, sex, cultural change, and native environment. It is not related to age or the type of organization in which the respondent works. The pattern for bureaucratic variables is identical to that which was found for the efficiency index with the exception of time in the public service, which has a strong influence on innovation scores but no discernible effect on efficiency scores. For nonbureaucratic variables considerable differences in patterns were observed. Lower class origin in particular seems to have a positive effect upon efficiency scores and a negative effect upon innovation scores. The location of the respondents' infancy and adolesence had this effect in one location (the Andes) but not in others.

The difference or similarity of native regions and job locations does not influence innovation scores as much as the native region alone. Whether working in Caracas or the interior, native Caraqueños averaged higher innovation scores than any other group (17 with an *n* of 51 for the former and 22 with an *n* of 7 for the latter). Those respondents raised in the interior averaged 11 when working in Caracas (38 respondents) and 13 when working in the interior (20 respondents). Those with mixed backgrounds averaged 16 ($n = 20$) when working in Caracas and only 7 ($n = 10$) when working in the interior. This last finding strongly supports the idea that the interior is more traditional in authority relations than the metropolis.

It is in the general area of background variables, in fact, where the greatest differences between efficiency and innovation score patterns appear. From this we could argue either that innovation is the more "modern" value and therefore more likely to be found in the city (Lerner's thesis) or that personal authority relations are simply more important in the interior than in Caracas. The effect of both hypotheses will be the same, although the first emphasizes the aggregate and the second the individual.

It will be remembered that the average respondent was reluctant to maintain efficiency criteria when doing so would have a negative effect upon his colleagues. In other words, personal criteria are deeply ingrained and often more important than administrative criteria to our respondents. In authority relationships those two criteria coincide: the traditionally authoritarian relationships of the Venezuelan family support the administrative value of hierarchy. Efficiency concerns are less directly bound up with personal relations and therefore more easily accepted than innovation in authority relations.

While it is certainly an arguable thesis that background factors such as the family have primary effects upon administrative values (after all, job levels remain the most powerful indicators of both efficiency and innovation scores), it would seem to be worth investigation. Prismatic theory emphasizes that man exists in a polynormative world, and certainly family ties and responsibilities are important to men.

The logic here leads to the assumption that the Andino's low average score is the result of being raised in a very traditional family, while the relatively high scores of the Caraqueños are a result of the looser or less authoritarian family ties in the metropolis. The following chapter concentrates upon family ties and responsibilities as they are perceived by the respondents, in an attempt to relate these to the bureaucratic and personal variables already discussed. An effort is also made to oppose personal and administrative criteria in order to gain some understanding of the respondents' priorities among the values often present in administrative decisions.

VIII.

PERSONAL PRIORITIES AND POLYNORMATIVE CHOICE

Prismatic theory is based upon the fundamental assumption that man is not unidimensional. Rather he is multidimensional, with different roles to play in society and competing norms for these roles. In rare cases a man may be presented with a choice that involves only one value and may be understood completely using only one norm. The more usual case, however, is that of choice which involves many norms, each of which implies more or less different decisions. That is, man exists in a polynormative world, and his actions cannot usually be understood through the use of a single norm. Even when the norms involved are mutually supportive rather than contrary or contradictory, the ultimate decision is almost always different from that which would have resulted from the use of only one norm. Fanaticism may be defined in these terms as the use of only one norm to judge all choices, and most men are not fanatics.

The situation is exacerbated when society is undergoing basic change. We have earlier described this sort of society as "transitional" and identified Venezuela as a transitional nation. One basic unit of society involved in this change is the family. In an effort to establish the strength of both the extended family and the nuclear family to our respondents we have constructed an index from questions involving the perceived priorities of family loyalties and responsibilities. Strong extended families are thought to be characteristic of traditional societies, and nuclear families of "modern" societies. This is surely a question of degree rather than of kind, and these values have clear application to our study when they come in contact with the bureaucratic world.

Our first objective in this chapter is to investigate the relative priorities that our respondents feel exist towards their relatives and friends. We have attempted to do this by presenting the respondents with statements on personal priorities and obligations (Table 22). An index of the same sort derived from the efficiency and innovation items has been constructed. The range of the resulting "personal priority" scores proved to be half again as large as that for the efficiency and innovation scores (100 to −54 as opposed to ranges of 100 on the previous indices), with a larger standard deviation (26). This indicates that the respondents were more agreed about norms in the bureaucratic world than they were about the more personal (and perhaps more basic) world of family relations.

Furthermore, while the average score was almost exactly the same as for the efficiency index (35 vs. 36) the distribution of scores was negatively skewed more than the other two indices (−.46 as opposed to −.14 and −.06). The skewness is still not great, however, and the distribution is essentially a rather flat normal curve.

As with the other indices, our interest is not with the absolute values involved but with the relative scores of different subgroups of our respondents. Even so, the questions are of interest in themselves because they can tell us something of the respondents.

There seems to have been a basic distinction made between the extended family consisting of a man and all his relatives, and the nuclear family of a man, his wife, and their children. The two items least agreed with on the scale, for instance, have to do with the extended family (items 12 and 13). It is clear that the overwhelming majority of our respondents (82 percent) reject the idea that the extended family should have their first allegiance. They also reject the idea that these relations should be among their first priorities by 55 percent, but this is a much reduced majority. Whether or not the extended family was paramount in historic Venezuela, it does not seem to be so for the majority of our respondents.

On the other hand, the nuclear family is more important than any other responsibility for 85 percent of our respondents (item 5) and only one percent disagreed with the idea that the nuclear family is among a man's most important responsibilities (item 1). When responsibilities towards the nuclear family were put in the negative (item 4) 89 percent of the respondents rejected the item, indicating that nuclear family responsibility is a value consistently held by our respondents.

Sixty-five percent or more of our respondents have agreed with each of the first eleven items in the scale, indicating that in general family and friendship ties are highly valued. An absolute statement upon the mutual responsibilities of close friends received more than 90 percent agreement, as did a conditional statement

TABLE 22. Personal Priority Items

		%	Percentage agreeing with efficiency value
1. The responsibilities a man has to his wife and children are among the most important he has.	completely agree agree disagree completely disagree	62 35 1 0 (NR = 2)	92
2. A man should help his relatives when he can.	completely agree agree disagree completely disagree	33 60 5 1 (NR = 1)	93
3. Close friends should always help each other when help is needed.	completely agree agree disagree completely disagree	24 69 7 0 (NR = 0)	93
4. The responsibilities a man has to his wife and children are of only average importance.	completely disagree disagree agree completely agree	40 49 6 3 (NR = 2)	89
5. The responsibilities a man has to his wife and children should have priority over all his other responsibilities.	completely agree agree disagree completely disagree	44 41 12 1 (NR = 2)	85
6. A man should seek close friends because friends and a man's family give meaning to his life.	completely agree agree disagree completely disagree	20 59 19 1 (NR = 1)	79
7. A man should do everything possible to help his relatives.	completely agree agree disagree completely disagree	14 64 18 2 (NR = 2)	78
8. While work may be a necessity, personal relations are what give life its savor.	completely agree agree disagree completely disagree	21 50 25 3 (NR = 1)	71

TABLE 22. *continued*

		%	Percentage agreeing with efficiency value
9. A man should help his godchildren when they are beginning their careers.	completely agree	9	69
	agree	60	
	disagree	28	
	completely disagree	1 (NR = 0)	
10. The life of a man without close friends and without strong family ties is a life without value.	completely agree	28	67
	agree	39	
	disagree	26	
	completely disagree	5 (NR = 2)	
11. To have godchildren is an honor and a great responsibility because it is the duty of a godfather to help his godchildren whenever they need help.	completely agree	14	65
	agree	51	
	disagree	24	
	completely disagree	8 (NR = 3)	
12. A man's responsibilities to his relatives are among the most important that he has.	completely agree	10	43
	agree	33	
	disagree	50	
	completely disagree	5 (NR = 2)	
13. A man's responsibilities to his relatives should have priority over all his other responsibilities.	completely agree	1	14
	agree	13	
	disagree	67	
	completely disagree	15 (NR = 4)	

upon the extended family. A slightly less conditional item on extended family responsibilities met with correspondingly less approval. In the light of the reaction to the absolute statement of this value already described a clear pattern emerges: the extended family is of low priority importance to our respondents. Close friends and the nuclear family rank higher.

Relationships with godchildren, which may be viewed either as an extension of the family to close friends or a device to increase the individual's (or family's) influence and security, depending upon the intent of those involved, are not considered as important by the respondents as those with the nuclear family and friends. On the other hand, 65 percent agreed with an absolute statement on the duties of godfathers, so despite its rather low ranking (11 of 13) a majority of the respondents were willing to consider such a relation as binding. Two questions on the values of work or non-personal relations were resolved by the respondents in favor of personal values.

The picture that emerges from these thirteen items is one of a very strong orientation towards the nuclear family and close friends and an only slightly less strong orientation to the extended family, although an absolute commitment to the extended family was strongly rejected.

A basic question, of course, is how strong these values will prove to be when placed in opposition to bureaucratic values. In order to test for this eight choices were presented to our respondents in which personal and administrative values were present (Table 23). In seven of these situations family values were present and in six of them family and efficiency values were opposed. A hypothetical grandson or godson was increasingly in need of work but also increasingly unqualified for it. At the same time a nonfamily candidate for the position became better and better qualified. The respondent was asked to recommend one of the two candidates for the job.

The items in Table 23 are ranked according to the percentage of the respondents choosing personal values over administrative (i.e., those choosing the less qualified man for the job.). In the first two questions, however, this general condition does not apply, since the two candidates are stated to be equal in their qualifications. The only grounds for choosing one over the other are the personal considerations involved. Put another way, the only grounds for rejecting the family man and the grandson in these items would be a rejection of personal claims in the first case and of nepotism in the second. Neither presents a direct conflict with administrative efficiency. It is interesting, therefore, that 15 percent of the respondents chose the bachelor over the family man and 25 percent did not choose their grandson. These respondents may be considered to have rejected personal claims in favor of Weberian administrative values. (A nonresponse or choosing both candidate was considered a "personal" choice, since our primary interest is in the administrative values contained in the scale.)

At the opposite end of the scale 97 percent rejected their grandson when he was manifestly unfit for the position, even when he and his family desperately needed it. There are limits, apparently, beyond which our respondents will not go in discharging their family responsibilities.

Between these two extremes the results are more difficult to interpret. As long as we are concerned only with the "average" respondent, the results indicate that he would contravene administrative standards only when his grandson urgently needs a position. In fact, only a bare majority (52 percent) elected to recommend their grandson for the position he very much needed when he was unfit for promotion. Very nearly a majority (49 percent) chose their grandson when they had no information that he was in a crisis situation and the other candidate was better qualified.

Godsons very clearly do not have the same claims upon the respondents as grandsons in the same situation. Moreover, only 28 percent of the respondents chose their godson when the unknown candidate had the best qualifications. In an analogous situation where a grandson was definitely much less qualified (being able to do only acceptable work) but needed the job, 52 percent chose their grandson.

The questions in Table 23, then, are ranked according to a mixture of personal and administrative criteria. Ranked on the strength of personal need, for example, a value clearly relevant to our respondents, item 8 would rank ahead of the rest. Since our primary interest in this study is in administrative criteria, and we are concerned only secondarily with personal values, the arrangement indicated in the table by the numbers in parentheses forms the basis for the administrative/personal (a/p) scale. Low numbers indicate questions in which the "personal" candidate is as qualified as the "administrative" and higher numbers those in which he is less qualified. The number of the item in this arrangement indicates the degree to which the respondent will go in contravening administrative criteria. Thus a low a/p score is positive for administrative values and a high score negative.

The distribution of the respondents on the a/p scale (Table 24) indicates that there are three "sticking points" at which our respon-

TABLE 23. Administrative/Personal Items

In the following situations which candidate would you recommend for a job?

1. Candidate A and B are equal in all their qualifications, but candidate B is a bachelor while A has a wife and four children. (1)	Personal Administrative	(A) (B)	85% 12 (NR = 3)
2. Candidates A and B are equal in all their qualifications, but candidate B is your grandson. (2)	Personal Administrative	(B) (A)	74 22 (NR = 4)
3. Candidate B has the best qualifications, but is unknown and a bachelor, while A is your grandson and has your confidence and, moreover, has a wife and children. You know that your grandson urgently needs a job. (6)	Personal Administrative	(A) (B)	61 37 (NR = 2)
4. Candidate A has the best qualifications while candidate B can only do acceptable work. You don't know candidate A, but B is your grandson and needs a job because he is unemployed and has a wife and children. Your grandson has your confidence and is a good worker. (7)	Personal Administrative	(B) (A)	52 46 (NR = 2)
5. Candidate B is a little better qualified than candidate A, but is unknown, while A is your grandson and, moreover, an honest person. (4)	Personal Administrative	(A) (B)	49 48 (NR = 3)
6. Candidate A is a little better qualified than candidate B, but B is your godson and, moreover, you know he is an honest person. (3)	Personal Administrative	(B) (A)	38 59 (NR = 3)

TABLE 23. *continued*

7. Candidate A has the best quali- fications but is unknown, while B is your godson and has your your confidence. (5)	Personal Administrative	(B) (A)	28 68 (NR = 4)
8. Candidate B has the best quali- fications of all who have applied for the job. Candidate A is your grandson but is an alcoholic and a scoundrel. Nevertheless, he has a wife and small children and the job would resolve a family problem, since the family is presently in a difficult situation. (8)	Personal Administrative	(A) (B)	3 97 (NR = 0)

dents tend to bunch. The distribution is not, consequently, a normal distribution and the measures used for the previous scales are not appropriate. The first point at which a substantial number of our respondents balk is item 3, where the first conflict between personal and administrative norms is found. Objections to personal criteria (item 1) and to nepotism as such (item 2) took precedence over personal criteria for only 4 percent of the respondents, but 15 percent more would not choose the "personal" candidate when such a choice would entail not recommending the more qualified candidate for the job (item 3, and the consequent a/p score of 2). That is, 19 percent of the respondents followed administrative efficiency criteria exclusively in responding to these items.

If this point was passed, the next sticking point for most respondents was choosing a candidate who was clearly unfit for promo-

TABLE 24. Distribution of Respondents According to
Administrative/Personal Scores

	0	1	2	3	4	5	6	7	8
Percentage	1	3	15	2	5	—	19	51	3
of respondents	(2)	(5)	(23)	(3)	(8)	(0)	(29)	(78)	(5)

tion (item 7, an a/p score of 6). Those who made an a/p score of 7 (the third, and most common, sticking point) indicated their willingness to recommend such a relative, but were not willing to recommend their grandson when he was an alcoholic and a scoundrel. Those were willing to do so attained an a/p score of 8.

The a/p score does not indicate how many questions had been answered with the "administrative" choice before the last "personal choice." An "ambiguity" scale was devised to indicate the number of these choices. It is important to remember, of course, that these responses are only "ambiguous" with reference to administrative and personal criteria when these criteria are considered separately. There is nothing particularly ambiguous in contravening administrative criteria in favor of personal criteria only after a certain degree of need has been passed if the two criteria are considered together. In prismatic terms such a situation is normal. People in any society are rarely faced with situations that can be judged by only one value.

As an example of the use of the ambiguity scale, a respondent who recommended his grandson for a job when he needed one even though he was unfit for promotion, but did not do so when he was an alcoholic and a scoundrel would score 7 on the a/p scale. If the same respondent would not recommend either his grandson or his godson when they were not in a crisis situation and more qualified candidates were available (items 5, 6, and 7), but did use personal criteria for selection when qualifications were not an issue (items 1 and 2) the ambiguity score would be 3. An ambiguity score of 0 would indicate that the respondent had been entirely consistent with one or the other of the criteria involved until his particular sticking point was reached. Such a situation is not unusual, 40 percent of the respondents attaining this score (Table 25).

The object of the a/p and ambiguity scales is to provide a check upon the personal priority scores derived from Table 22. In that table personal values were cast in the abstract: here they are opposed to administrative values. The average a/p score was 5.6 and the average ambiguity score was 1.4, indicating that most respondents were entirely guided in their recommendations by neither criteria.

A division of personal priority, ambiguity, and a/p scores by job levels (Table 26) reveals that while both department heads and non-

TABLE 25. Distribution of the Respondents on the Ambiguity Scale

Number of "Inconsistent" Responses

	0	1	2	3	4	5	6	7
Percentage	40	19	12	17	8	3	1	—
of respondents	(62)	(29)	(18)	(26)	(13)	(4)	(1)	(0)

TABLE 26. Personal Priority, Administrative/Personal, Ambiguity, Efficiency, and Innovation Scores by Job Levels

	Personal Priority	a/p	Ambiguity	Efficiency	Innovation
Department Heads (16)	38	4.6	1.2	43	24
Division or Section Heads (80)	32	5.6	1.4	36	13
Nonchiefs (57)	38	5.8	1.6	34	12

Note: For purposes of comparison all the indices will be included in all the tables in this chapter.

command respondents had higher personal priority scores than division or section heads, these values did not directly effect the corresponding a/p ambiguity scores. Abstract personal priorities rank higher for high command and noncommand positions than for middle level respondents (a bimodal distribution), but when administrative and personal values are placed in opposition a linear relationship emerges: the higher the command level, the stronger the administrative norms and the less ambiguous they are. This would indicate that administrative norms become stronger as higher command levels are reached, regardless of the individual's commitment to personal values. It will be recalled that efficiency and innovation scores followed this pattern rather than the nonlinear distribution of the personal priority scores.

If scores are broken down by line and staff distinctions as well as job levels (Tables 27 and 28) it becomes obvious that the high personal priority scores of the high and low job levels are a function

TABLE 27. All Indices by Line Job Level

	Personal Priority	a/p	Ambiguity	Efficiency	Innovation
Department Heads (9)	32	4.3	1.4	45	26
Division or Section Heads (41)	31	5.7	1.5	36	14
Nonchiefs	34	6.3	1.3	30	8

TABLE 28. All Indices by Staff Job Levels

	Personal Priority	a/p	Ambiguity	Efficiency	Innovation
Department Heads (7)	46	5.0	1.0	42	22
Division or Section Heads (30)	33	5.5	1.3	36	12
Nonchiefs (39)	40	5.6	1.7	36	13

of the high staff scores on these job levels. Line respondents are essentially the same on all levels for this criteria. On the other hand, a/p scores for the two kinds of work have the same distribution pattern with two important differences: line department heads average much lower and line noncommand respondents much higher than their staff counterparts. This parallels almost exactly the patterns found with efficiency and innovation scores.

As a general rule ambiguity scores rise and fall with a/p scores. In one sense this is a function of the measure, since an ambiguity score by definition cannot be higher than one less than the a/p score. This makes the ambiguity score of the line noncommand respondents all the more remarkable, for it is only average, while their a/p score is very high. That is, they are willing to contravene administrative norms in almost all the imagined situations and are no more ambiguous than the average group almost a full point below them. They are in fact less ambiguous than line department heads, even though the latter group is two full points below them on the a/p scale. This result is consistent with the analysis of efficiency and innovation scores, which was that line noncommand respondents were relatively unconcerned with either of these values. We can now add that they consistently choose personal over administrative criteria in situations in which the two conflict and that they are relatively unambiguous in doing so.

Line department heads show the opposite pattern, although they too exhibit an average ambiguity rate. Staff department heads, on the other hand, are less ambiguous with a higher a/p score, although the latter is still less than the average for all respondents. Why staff department heads and noncommand respondents have personal priority scores so much higher than the average is not answerable from the data.

A division of the respondents by age (Table 29) indicates that older and younger respondents have higher personal priority and a/p scores than respondents in the intermediate age groups. In both cases the youngest respondents had the highest scores on these variables yet recorded, as well as the highest ambiguity rate. Conversely, the intermediate groups had the lowest personal priority and a/p scores, those thirty-one to thirty-three years old having the lowest personal priority score yet recorded. Even so, the a/p score of this age group was almost a full point higher than that attained by line department heads. Again, personal priority scores and the measure we have devised to test the strength of these values in administrative situations do not seem to have a direct connection.

Neither efficiency nor innovation scores showed any consistent pattern by age groups. There is strong evidence, however, that personal priority scores vary with age, those in their middle years

TABLE 29. All Indices by Age Groups

	Personal Priority	a/p	Ambiguity	Efficiency	Innovations
39 and over *(28)*	39	5.5	1.2	38	14
34–38 *(25)*	32	4.9	1.2	38	11
31–33 *(41)*	26	5.2	1.5	35	14
28–30 *(31)*	34	5.8	1.3	36	18
Less than 28 *(28)*	47	6.5	1.9	34	11

being less committed to personal ties than those who are older or younger. There is no linear relationship between age and personal priority scores at all ($r = -.01$).

Much the same pattern appears in the a/p scores as in the personal priority scores, except that the low point has moved up one age bracket and the lowest average score is not as low as the previous low (4.3 by line department heads). This is reflected in very weak negative linear correlations with age for a/p and ambiguity scores (a/p $= -.19$, ambiguity $= -.13$).

A division by time in the public service (Table 30) reveals much the same nonlinear correlations as were found by age groups. Here, however, those respondents with from six to nine years in the public service have the lowest personal priority, a/p, and ambiguity scores, whereas with age groups these attributes were shared by two or more groups. Furthermore, this seniority group also had the highest innovation score. With the exception of efficiency scores, a very strong nonlinear pattern is evident in this table: those respondents with six to nine years in the public service are more positively oriented towards administrative criteria, less positively oriented towards personal criteria, and less ambiguous when they must choose between the two criteria than any other group.

TABLE 30. All Indices by Seniority Groups

Years in the Public Service	Personal Priority	a/p	Ambiguity	Efficiency	Innovation
14–Highest (29)	41	5.4	1.3	37	7
10–13 (34)	29	5.4	1.5	35	14
6–9 (32)	25	4.9	1.1	36	20
3–5 (34)	39	6.1	1.6	33	14
Less than 3 (24)	43	6.2	1.6	33	13

Another interesting aspect of the table is that both less and more seniority tends to increase personal considerations and decrease administrative concerns, although this tendency is much more pronounced with newer personnel. This is evidence that a rather strong socialization in administrative norms take place, for all of the various indices indicate that those respondents with the least seniority are the least in favor of administrative criteria. With innovation scores, however, the most senior group attained the lowest score. This value seems to be more sharply affected by extended experience than the others. The general import of Table 30 is that attitudes towards administrative values are strongly affected by time in the public service and that this effect is nonlinear.

Differences by sex (Table 31) are apparent but not particularly significant. None of the scores are very far from the average, and the differences between scores are not great, particularly for the personal priority, a/p and ambiguity indices. Perhaps the most important aspect of this table is that it confirms the earlier conclusion derived from the efficiency and innovation scores: women are not more oriented towards personal criteria and less towards administrative criteria than men. If anything, the opposite is true. Even when the two criteria were placed in opposition, women were less willing to contravene administrative criteria than men. Furthermore, they had higher ambiguity scores even though their a/p scores were lower, indicating a stronger propensity to choose administrative criteria even if that propensity can be overridden by family considerations in crisis situations.

TABLE 31. All Indices by Sex of Respondent

	Personal Priority	a/p	Ambiguity	Efficiency	Innovation
Men (113)	36	5.7	1.3	35	12
Women (40)	31	5.3	1.7	40	17

A split by the type of organization in which the respondents work indicated that the respondents are not sharply differentiated by this division. The idea that the nonministerial organizations are not very different from the older institutions is supported by this finding.

The thesis that conditions of work are different in the interior from those in Caracas and that therefore attitudes will also be different receives support from a division along these lines (Table 32), but the

TABLE 32. All Indices by Job Location

	Personal Priority	a/p	Ambiguity	Efficiency	Innovation
Caracas (114)	36	5.4	1.2	34	14
Interior (39)	32	6.0	2.1	42	14

conclusions to be drawn from these differences are conflicting. On the one hand, interior respondents value efficiency highly, giving support to the hypothesis that they suffer more from the effects of centralization than those working in the central city. On the other hand, the interior respondents are more willing to contravene administrative criteria for family interests, even though they have a lower personal priority score than their counterparts in Caracas. Their high ambiguity score indicates that such a contravention would occur only when the need of the family member is great, however, and perhaps the best conclusion that can be drawn from the table is that both efficiency concerns and family need are likely to be higher in the interior. Certainly the idea that interior respondents will be more "traditional" than those in the metropolis finds no support in this data.

An investigation of the effects of urban or nonurban childhood environment on the variables under discussion (Table 33) yields interesting results. The personal priority scores are again a mirror

TABLE 33. All Indices by Infant and Adolescent Environments
        of Respondents

	Personal Priority	a/p	Ambiguity	Efficiency	Innovation
Urban (116)	33	5.7	1.6	37	14
Rural, Small Town and Rural/Small Town (21)	45	5.8	1.1	32	8
Rural/Urban and Small Town/ Urban (16)	31	4.4	0.9	37	21

image of the innovation scores, as they were with time in the public service, and the efficiency scores are also the reverse of the personal priority scores. A completely nonurban childhood environment is associated with high personal priority scores, low ambiguity and efficiency scores, and very low innovation scores. Respondents from urban environments are associated with the opposite pattern on these variables, as are those from mixed backgrounds, but the mixed-background respondents are more extreme on all measures except efficiency than the completely urban. Here again the data support the conclusion that a mixed urban/nonurban childhood environment is most strongly associated with "modern" traits. This is especially clear when a/p scores are examined. Here respondents from both urban and nonurban environments produce essentially the same scores—slightly above average. The only difference is that urban respondents tend to be more ambiguous on this scale than their nonurban colleagues.

Those with a mixed background are a full point below the average on the a/p scale and even less ambiguous than the completely nonurban respondents. This, coupled with the high innovation scores associated with a mixed urban/nonurban background, is a strong indication that the "modern" traits that concern us here are more closely associated with cultural change than with either culture by itself. Lerner's theory continues to hold in its negative phase: those with completely nonurban backgrounds are consistently associated with "nonmodern" traits. Even so, when a choice was forced between administrative and personal criteria, there was no real difference between respondents from unmixed backgrounds. Only a culturally mixed background has resulted in our respondents' attaining a low score on this variable.

Dividing the respondents according to specific geographic locations again reveals quite different patterns for the different groups involved (Table 34). Disregarding those groups with fewer than ten respondents, the Caraqueños, Andinos, other Venezuelans, and those who grew up both in Caracas and non-Andean Venezuela all demonstrate that no single-factor theory is adequate to explain the differences. Caraqueños, for instance, score relatively high on the efficiency and innovation scales, average on ambiguities, and relatively low on personal priorities. Up to this point the pattern is quite plain: an emphasis upon administrative criteria is associated with a deemphasis of family ties. The trouble with this theory is

TABLE 34. All Indices by Place of Respondents' Infancy
            and Adolescence

	Personal Priority	a/p	Ambiguity	Efficiency	Innovation
Caracas (58)	32	5.8	1.4	38	18
Andes (17)	43	4.4	1.1	38	11
Other Venezuelan (41)	39	6.0	1.5	35	12
Foreign (7)	32	5.1	1.0	41	1
Caracas/Andes (5)	34	5.0	1.6	42	12
Caracas/Other Venezuelan (24)	31	5.5	1.8	28	14
Caracas/Foreign (1)	15	7.0	0.0	46	0

that it cannot account for the high a/p scores achieved by the Caraqueños. It appears that when Caraqueños are forced to choose between personal and administrative criteria they frequently act upon the personal.

Andinos, on the other hand, show the contrary pattern: high personal and low innovation scores. Their efficiency scores are the same as those of the previous group, however, and despite their high personal scores they are much less willing to contravene administrative criteria than the Caraqueños and are less ambiguous about it. Their low a/p scores are lower, in fact, than any except those of line department heads (4.3) and are equaled only by those from mixed urban/nonurban backgrounds. Traditional wisdom would seem to be accurate in attributing strong family ties to Andinos, but the assumption that these ties interfere with their administrative acts appears to be inaccurate. On the other hand, Andinos have below average innovation scores, which would indicate that they largely accept the traditional authority system. This line of reasoning would argue that family and friendship are separable from efficiency concerns but that they have more durable associations with authority relations.

This argument is supported by the attitudes and choices of

those respondents raised in Venezuela but not in Caracas or the Andes. This group also couples a relatively high personal priority score with below average innovation scores but repeats the Caracas pattern of average efficiency scores and high a/p scores. That is, personal and innovation scores here seem related while choice and efficiency scores are not.

Finally, those respondents raised in both Caracas and non-Andean Venezuela couple average a/p and innovation scores with slightly above average ambiguity scores. Clearly, no single-factor theory is adequate to explain all these variations, although there does seem to be a fairly strong inverse relation between personal and innovation scores.

A division of the respondents by their fathers' native regions revealed that in general the same patterns exist here as those for the division according to respondent's native region, with the equally general condition that the majority of the scores are nearer the average than those in Table 34.

There are, however, three major exceptions to these generalizations: (1) the children of Andinos have above average innovation scores where native Andean respondents had lower than average innovation scores; (2) the children of Caraqueños have below average efficiency scores, while the average efficiency score of all those raised in Caracas is above average; and (3) the children of Caraqueños average very low personal priority scores when the same scores for all the respondents raised in Caracas were only slightly above average. Residence in Caracas for two generations seems to lower the felt need for strong family ties but does not lessen the extent to which these respondents are willing to contravene administrative criteria in the interests of the family. The basic implication of the two regional tables is (again) that cultural change, here exemplified in geographic mobility, is more influential in changing attitudes towards administrative criteria than continued residence in the regions themselves.

Social class and social mobility are cross-cutting variables that may be more influential than the nature or location of native environments. When the respondents are divided by perceived social class, the same patterns emerge that were seen in the case of innovation and efficiency scores. The only sizable groups (the middle and upper middle class respondents) are much the same on all the scales. When lower middle class respondents are considered, there

TABLE 35. All Indices by Fathers' Social Class

	Personal Priority	a/p	Ambiguity	Efficiency	Innovation
Upper Class (1)	38	7.0	4.0	29	22
Upper Middle Class (22)	36	4.8	1.1	39	14
Middle Class (78)	34	5.6	1.3	36	15
Lower Middle Class (41)	32	6.0	1.9	25	12
Lower Class (11)	51	5.4	0.9	42	10

does seem to be a definite trend towards unambiguous, nonad-ministrative values and a corresponding drop in administrative concerns, but the number involved is very small.

A divison by the respondents' fathers' social class (Table 35) in-dicates that within the middle class there is a tendency for personal priority, efficiency, and innovation scores to drop with social class, and a simultaneous rise in a/p and ambiguity scores. The differ-ences in personal priority and innovation scores are quite small, but the changes in the other three variables are large. Here again there seems to be an inverse relation between a/p scores and effi-ciency scores.

The eleven respondents who reported having lower class fathers have average a/p scores and above average efficiency scores, a result that is contrary to the thesis just developed for respondents with middle class fathers. Moreover, the ambiguity rate for the former group is quite low, whereas that of the latter is relatively high. The inverse relationship earlier noted between personal priorities and innovation scores is apparent in the group with lower class fathers. What is mainly apparent, however, is a very strong difference on all variables except innovation and perhaps a/p scores between those with lower class fathers and those with lower middle class fathers.

Social change over two generations thus seems more powerful than social class by itself. A division along these lines indicates that no major differences exist between those respondents who have achieved upward mobility and those who have maintained the same class as their fathers. That is, movement from the lower class is much more significant than upward mobility in general.

Status deprivation is more powerful than any of the previous social distinctions in its effect upon innovation and personal priority scores. The previously observed inverse relationship of these variables is particularly strong here. Status deprivation is also associated with an indifferent efficiency score, a below average a/p score, and a very low ambiguity score. The major effect of status deprivation, however, is upon innovation and personal priorities.

Graduate education judged by the location of the graduate school (Table 36) reveals no marked disparity from the patterns noted earlier. The respondents who report graduate training in non-Venezuelan Latin American schools again have unusual scores but are too few to allow generalization. Those with no graduate school education

TABLE 36. All Indices by Location of Respondent's Graduate School

	Personal Priority	a/p	Ambiguity	Efficiency	Innovation
No Graduate School (123)	34	5.6	1.4	35	14
Venezuelan Graduate School (18)	38	5.5	1.6	37	10
European or North American Graduate School (9)	39	4.9	1.4	45	21
Latin American Graduate School (2)	46	4.5	0.5	40	39

are average on every scale. Venezuelan graduate students are not very different from those respondents who lack graduate training, although they are as much higher on the personal priority scale as they are lower than the average in innovation. The respondents with graduate training in Europe or North America have below average a/p and personal priority scores and are average on the ambiguity scale. As noted earlier, they are much higher than the

Venezuelan graduate students and the nongraduate students on the efficiency and innovation scales. The new information we have gained in this chapter would reinforce the idea previously expressed that they are less "traditional" than the Venezuelan groups, but there is still no way to differentiate between the effects of the selection process and the effects of the graduate schools themselves. It may be that only the most innovative and efficiency-oriented graduates of the Venezuelan universities seek or are given the opportunity to study abroad.

The second conclusion previously reached with regard to graduate training is also sustained: graduate training in Venezuela does not generally result in higher (or more "modern") scores on our scales, and particularly has a negative effect upon the innovation scores of these respondents.

A somewhat surprising result is that the highest personal priority score of any group (47) was attained by the 28 respondents in the youngest age group. It may be that people in this age group are more in need of the kind of help implied in the items that make up the personal priority scale, and therefore tend to approve of the family ties that might benefit them. Given this analysis, the fact that the 41 respondents thirty-one to thirty-three years old averaged only 26 points on this scale is rather dramatic. Only three other groups (those with fathers raised in foreign countries, those with from six to nine years' seniority in the public service, and those who reported being in a lower class than their fathers) averaged lower personal priority scores. The only intervening variable common to all the respondents that also resulted in major differences on this index is time in the public service. Those with less than three years' seniority averaged 43 on the personal priority index. While age appears to be a somewhat stronger factor here, the obvious question is which of the two factors influences the respondents more as they simultaneously grow older and gain in experience.

An answer to this question leads us to the a/p scores. The implication of the drop in personal priority scores with age is that bureaucratic factors have had a major impact upon the respondents. Increased time in the public service results in exceptionally low personal priority scores and also in low a/p scores. Those with less than three and from three to five years in the public service have very high a/p scores (6.2 and 6.1), being exceeded on this scale only by those who are less than 28 years old (6.5). Those who are thirty-four to thirty-eight years old and those with six to nine years in the public service, however, both averaged 4.9 on the a/p scale, a drop of 1.2 points on an 8-point scale. Other groups had lower a/p scores, but no other variable demonstrated such dramatic differences among its groups. It will be remembered that neither age nor seniority permanently affected these scores. After the low point was reached, subsequent age and seniority groups moved upwards on these scales until the initial levels were approximated.

Clearly, something has happened to our respondents during their first ten years in the public service. It may be that some sort of promotion crisis is reached between six and nine years after joining the bureaucracy that causes them to discount family ties, to emphasize administrative criteria over family responsibilities, and also to become above average in their positive concern for innovation. Perhaps the best explanation is that their socialization in bureaucratic norms and their ambitions to rise in the public service both tend to peak at about this time in their careers.

This explanation would discount background factors in favor of bureaucratic variables. It is supported by the low a/p scores attained by department heads (4.6, $n = 16$). Line department heads in particular place administrative criteria before personal considerations, averaging 4.3 ($n = 9$). They do not, however, exhibit the low personal priority scores that accompanied the younger respondents' attainment of low a/p scores. Staff department heads in particular averaged very high personal priority scores (46) and line department heads were only slightly below average (32). The implication is that these respondents do not need to discount personal responsibilities in order to give priority to their administrative responsibilities.

The idea that within an administrative context bureaucratic factors are more powerful than background factors, especially for those in mid-career and those who have recently been promoted, is further supported by the high a/p score (6.0) attained by the 39 respondents working in the interior. The explanation advanced to account for this group's high efficiency concern would seem to be inadequate here. If working conditions in the interior entail inefficient and frustrating relations with agency headquarters in Caracas, thus heightening the interior respondent's concerns with efficiency, it would seem inconsistent for these same respondents to contravene administrative criteria in favor of personal responsibilities. A cross-cutting factor may be that family pressures and necessities may be stronger in the interior than in the metropolis, and prismatic theory would hold that such a response is normal. When confronted with a polynormative situation, however, they opted for personal criteria over administrative but were highly ambiguous (2.1) in doing so. It is fairly clear that these respondents hold norms that they themselves would perceive as contrary.

So far bureaucratic factors have tended to predominate, but the scores of the interior respondents indicate that background variables may in some situations prove stronger. This is perhaps most clearly seen when job locations are considered in conjunction with the respondent's native region (Table 37). Efficiency scores correlated best with job location, while innovation scores tended to be highest when respondents were working outside the region where they grew up. When they had mixed backgrounds or were raised in foreign countries, job location became the deciding factor. Personal priority scores followed neither pattern, demonstrating no fixed criteria for prediction. The a/p scores, however, demonstrate a rather strong pattern associating a change from native region to job location with lower scores. Those with mixed or foreign backgrounds, on the other hand, tend to have higher scores when stationed in the interior.

The data on polynormative choice, when considered with the other dependent variables, has supported the prismatic notion that competing forms for behavior are held by our respondents and that situational factors are important in determining which norms will receive priority when the respondents must act in a polynormative situation. Bureaucratic factors, especially job level, have been found to have the highest predictive values, but below the highest job levels other variables, both bureaucratic and nonbureaucratic, have often been found stronger.

Status deprivation, for example, seems to have had a profound effect upon the few respondents who report it. In such cases, very low personal priority, a/p, and ambiguity scores are associated with very high innovation scores. Hagen's thesis that status deprivation causes "modernizing" attitudes in those who experience it would seem to be sustained. Lerner's thesis, on the other hand, does not seem to be justified in the light of our data. Simple residence in an urban setting is not associated with the values we have considered

TABLE 37. All Indices by Job Location and Native Origin

	Personal Priority	a/p	Ambiguity	Efficiency	Innovation
Those raised in Caracas, working in Caracas (51)	35	5.9	1.4	37	17
Those raised in interior, working in Caracas (38)	40	5.1	1.0	32	38
Those raised in interior, working in interior (20)	40	6.2	1.0	44	13
Those raised in Caracas, working in interior (7)	8	5.0	1.6	44	22
Those from mixed backgrounds, working in Caracas (20)	29	4.9	1.4	29	16
Those from mixed backgrounds, working in interior (10)	35	6.5	2.4	34	7
Those raised in foreign countries, working in Caracas (5)	37	5.0	0.2	36	−7
Those raised in foreign countries, working in interior (2)	19	5.5	3.0	52	22

"modern," and two generations of residence in Caracas, one of the most cosmopolitan cities in the world, has resulted in below average innovation scores, the most change-oriented of our measures.

On the other hand, a nonurban background did result in very "traditional" attitudes, so Lerner's thesis seems to be correct in its negative implications. More importantly, we have consistently found high innovation and efficiency scores associated with cultural change, in both bureaucratic and nonbureaucratic situations. The openness to change and different ways of doing things that seem to result from cultural change are not, however, transferable across generations nor are they necessarily accompanied by high concerns for efficiency.

Efficiency concerns, in fact, seem to be associated with a willingness to accept family responsibilities. High personal priority scores and high efficiency scores have often occurred together in our tables, and it may be that these are measures more of a general willingness to be responsible than of anything else. In order to follow this theme further, however, we must investigate the relations among our indices.

IX.

A COMPARISON OF THE INDICES

A major question, of course, is whether or not efficiency and innovation scores are closely related. As far as a simple linear relationship goes, they are not, although there is a relatively weak positive
correlation between the two (Pearson's $r = .39$). A breakdown of
average innovation scores by efficiency levels (Table 38) reveals
that the second factor has no effect upon the first. The reverse table
(Table 39) indicates that innovation levels do have a slight effect on
efficiency scores, but that this relation is not linear. Respondents

TABLE 38. Innovation Averages by Efficiency Levels		TABLE 39. Efficiency Averages by Innovation Levels	
Efficiency Level	Innovation Average	Innovation Level	Efficiency Average
High (56)	14	High (54)	39
Medium (50)	14	Medium (51)	31
Low (47)	14	Low (48)	39

who are substantially above average on the efficiency index tend to
have extreme rather than moderate attitudes towards innovation,
and the degree of this tendency is equal in both directions. Above
average efficiency scores are associated with both high and low
innovation levels. Those of our respondents who are strongly oriented towards efficiency may accept or reject innovation as a primary value in administration, but they are unlikely to be neutral
about it.

When innovation levels are crossed with efficiency levels a random distribution results. The same process repeated for subgroups
reveals that department heads and low-level line respondents have
a more or less strong tendency to associate the two criteria. All other
groups that proved to have significant connections with either one

or the other of the two scales did not show any significant evidence of a connection between the two. It would seem that as the most responsible hierarchical levels are reached our respondents tend to become positively oriented to both these values. Below these levels our respondents do not make any consistent connections between efficiency and innovation criteria, with the exception of the line noncommand respondents, who tend to reject them both.

Personal priority scores have a weak positive correlation with efficiency scores ($r = .21$) and an equally weak negative correlation with innovation scores ($r = -.26$). The first finding would support the supposition that our respondents have a tendency to become more responsible administrators as they accept their responsibilities within their families. The weakness of the relation and the previous evidence that at least some of our groups do not seem to make such a connection render such an assumption highly tentative, but in polynormative situations it would explain the frequent occurrence of the positive association of the two scores.

When personal priority scores are broken down by efficiency levels (Table 40), it becomes clear that only those respondents who are highly concerned with efficiency have an equally strong belief in family responsibilities. Those not highly concerned with efficiency are indistinguishable on the personal priority index. When efficiency scores are broken down by personal priority scores (Table 41), a weak but definite pattern is revealed: higher concerns with family responsibilities are associated with higher concerns for administrative efficiency. This would, of course, support the idea that family relations are the more basic of the two criteria.

TABLE 40. Personal Priority Averages by Efficiency Levels

Efficiency Level	Personal Priority Average
High (56)	42
Medium (50)	31
Low (47)	31

TABLE 41. Efficiency Averages by Personal Priority Levels

Personal Priority Level	Efficiency Average
High (57)	39
Medium (47)	36
Low (49)	32

Innovation levels prove to have the opposite effect upon personal priority averages from those that personal priority levels have upon efficiency scores (Table 42). The same pattern exists when innovation scores are broken down by personal priority levels (Table 43). A probable explanation is that innovation, as we have used it in our index, involves changes in personal and hierarchical authority relations. More delegation of authority and more trust in subordinates, as well as a more general belief that new ways of doing things are needed, are involved. The personal priority index emphasizes responsibilities within the nuclear and extended family.

TABLE 42. Personal Priority Averages by Innovation Levels		TABLE 43. Innovation Averages by Personal Priority Levels	
Innovation Levels	*Personal Priority Averages*	*Personal Priority Levels*	*Innovation Averages*
High (54)	29	High (57)	9
Medium (51)	34	Medium (47)	12
Low (48)	42	Low (49)	22

That is, it in one sense measures the respondents' acceptance of the traditional Venezuelan family. Since authority within the traditional family has been located in the head of the family on a personal and direct basis, the personal priority scale may in this sense be considered an indirect measure of the respondents' acceptance of the responsibilities and privileges of traditional positions of authority. This would explain both the negative correlation with innovation and the weaker positive correlation with efficiency norms. In the first case traditional attitudes would lead to the rejection of change in authority relations, and in the second the acceptance of responsibilities in the family would be associated with the acceptance of responsibilities in the public service. The implications for administrative reform seem plain. Insofar as the situation described does in fact exist, increased efficiency and increased innovation will be incompatible goals.

The a/p scores were not significantly affected by efficiency levels, although there was a slight tendency for those who were neither high nor low on the efficiency scale to average higher ambiguity scores. This is consistent with the general idea that extreme attitudes reduce the tendency to judge situations by two or more of the norms involved rather than by a single norm.

The respondents were divided in accordance with the "sticking points" ($n = 30$) on the a/p scale in order to obtain levels on the scale. Those rated "low" ($n = 30$) achieved a score of 2 or lower, indicating that they would not under any conditions follow personal criteria if this entailed recommending a less qualified person. The "medium" category ($n = 40$) consists of those who scored between 3 and 6, indicating that they would recommend a less qualified person when he was not clearly unqualified. The "high" category ($n = 78$) is made up of those respondents who recommended their grandson even though he was unfit for promotion, i.e., those who attained a score of 7. The "very high" category ($n = 5$) is made up of those respondents who recommended their grandson when they knew he was an alcoholic and a scoundrel.

There is a slight negative correlation ($r = -.11$) between efficiency scores and a/p scores, and when efficiency averages are run for a/p levels this finding is confirmed. High, medium, and low a/p levels averaged 35, 37, and 39 respectively on the efficiency scale, but while the direction is consistent the differences are not great. The very high group, however, averaged 18 on the efficiency scale. This reinforces the feeling that only the eighth item on the a/p scale indicated a really crucial difference for our respondents, regardless of their own particular sticking points.

When innovation and a/p levels are crossed no distinct differences are found, although a medium rating on both scales is associated with higher values on the other. There is no linear correlation between the two criteria at all ($r = -.02$). It would seem that for our respondents a concern with change in authority relations and whether or not one practices nepotism are completely different issues.

Crossing personal priority and a/p scores indicates that medium scores are again associated with differences in the other variable. Here medium concerns with family and friendship ties are related to somewhat lower a/p scores while medium levels of polynormative choice are related to slightly higher personal priority averages. What is more interesting, perhaps, is that those respondents who are very high on the a/p scale are the lowest on the personal priority scale. Evidently these respondents make a rather clear distinction between family ties in the abstract and family responsibility in particular cases. Conversely, this finding supports the thesis that the acceptance of family responsibilities and the acceptance of administrative responsibilities are closely linked for our respondents.

The nonlinear nature of what relationship there is between these variables is evident in their very low correlation index ($r = .04$). The tenuous nature of the relationship is so marked that we may consider these two variables unrelated for most of our respondents. Administrative criteria are more influential in a/p choice than personal criteria. Efficiency scores in particular are the best guides we have for predicting a/p scores.

Of all the combinations we have examined, personal priority scores and innovation scores seem to be the most closely related. Efficiency and innovation scores have a higher linear correlation, but the causation appears to be in one direction only. Efficiency levels have no effect upon innovation scores but high and low innovation levels are associated with above-average efficiency scores. The relation between personal priority scores and innovation scores is consistent across both tables. High innovation scores are associated with low levels of personal priority scores, and low personal priority scores are associated with high innovation levels.

In general, our indices have proved to have greater relations with independent variables than with each other. This is additional support for the view that the world of our respondents in both its administrative and personal aspects is polynormative, and that the best way to understand values important to administrative reform is to view them as relatively independent criteria within an administrative framework. The following chapter will examine some of the more important issues of administrative reform in Venezuela through the use of the scales developed for efficiency and innovation. These remain the most immediately applicable and the most important values for administrative reform that we have examined.

X.

PUBLIC CORPORATIONS, DECENTRALIZATION, AND ISLANDS OF REFORM

The relative efficiency of public corporations when compared to the ministries, the decentralization of decision making within organizations, and the "islands of reform" strategy of administrative reform are or have been of great interest to the Commission of Public Administration and are of equal interest to this study. The following sections deal with these questions and the opinions our respondents have of them.

As mentioned earlier, one method of decentralization that Venezuelan governments have used extensively in the last thirty years has been that of creating nonministerial organizations for specific developmental purposes. These organizations generally report directly to the president (although all are now nominally under the ministries) and have a high degree of organizational independence. An argument that can be made for this independence is that it allows a higher degree of efficiency to develop in these organizations than would be possible if they were located in the ministries as departments or divisions. This argument is based partly upon the idea that new organizations can start with a clean slate and partly upon the idea that they will be more flexible than the older organizations. Our respondents were asked their opinion on this in the following item (Table 44).

The respondents are about evenly divided, with a few more willing to be extremely positive than are willing to be negative with equal force. The balance is reflected in the relatively high number who did not respond (7). It is difficult to see how this question could be seen as threatening by the respondents, so it is probable that the nonresponses were occasioned more by indecision than by a refusal to answer. There is some indication that the more efficiency-minded of our respondents totally agreed with the item. Those who completely disagreed were also above average on the efficiency index, however, and there is perhaps more evidence for

TABLE 44. Efficiency of Public Corporations: Efficiency and
Innovation Averages by Response Category

		%	Efficiency Average	Innovation Average
One of the best methods	completely	15	46	10
for achieving economic	agree			
development is to create	agree	36	32	12
public corporations which	disagree	38	33	15
can evade the inefficiency of	completely	10	38	21
the older governmental	disagree			
organizations.	NR = 7			

the possibility that those more positively oriented towards efficiency are also more positive in their ideas on how to achieve it regardless of which side of this particular issue they believe is right.
The below-average efficiency scores of the respondents who opted
for nonextreme responses would tend to support this idea.

Innovation scores give a much clearer picture: the higher a person scored on the innovation index the more he disagreed with the
idea that public corporations are more efficient than "the older
governmental organizations." This would imply that the kind of
innovation tested by the innovation index has more to do with
internal organization than with an institution's external situation.
At the very least, these responses indicate that the simple creation
of public corporations is not considered an innovative act.

A division of responses by job levels and types indicates that the
two types of jobs are quite powerful indicators of the responses to
this item. Line respondents become more favorable to public corporations as their rank increases, while staff respondents have
exactly the opposite pattern (Table 45). Only one of the seven staff
heads agreed with the item, while five of the eight line department
heads did so (the remaining line department head did not respond
to this item). Division or section heads were about evenly split for
both types of jobs and noncommand respondents felt the reverse
of their department heads, although the staff respondents were
much more extreme in this split than the line respondents.

The respondents who would presumably be well informed about
efficiency of the public corporations are those who work in pub-

TABLE 45. Agreement with Item on the Efficiency of Public
Corporations by Job Level and Type

	Department Heads	Division or Section Heads	Nonchiefs	
Line	63	55	40	49%
	(9)	(41)	(18)	
Staff	14	47	60	15%
	(7)	(39)	(39)	

lic corporations. Restricting the definition of a public corporation
to organizations that actually have "corporation" as part of their
names and to state enterprises such as the national airline results
in 22 respondents who can be considered as members of "public
corporations." The term is usually understood rather more broadly
in Venezuela, so this definition would seem to insure the inclusion
only of those respondents who are clearly identified with those
institutions. Foundations, research institutions, banks, and other
autonomous institutions are sometimes thought of as corporations
and sometimes not, so by restricting our definition we are in effect
weighting the answers on the positive side. Of the "public corporation" respondents, 14 (67 percent) rejected the idea that public
corporations are more efficient than older governmental organizations.

The situation here seems to be that public corporations appear
more attractive on efficiency criteria than other types of governmental organizations mainly to those respondents who do not work in
them. Moreover, they do not seem to be considered innovative by
those of our respondents positively oriented towards innovation.

The Decentralization of Policy Making

It was mentioned earlier that while the Venezuelan public service
contains a great many independent organizations, a very few of
which are not based in Caracas, there has been very little decentralization on an internal basis. Almost all decisions are made by
the central office, and the central office is almost always in Caracas.

This is essentially a centralization of authority or, conversely, a refusal or inability to delegate authority to handle any but the most routine matters to those below the top command levels of the organization. The following question was designed to obtain the opinions of the respondents upon a possible change towards a decentralization of authority (Table 46). This item is an extension of some of the items that made up the innovation scale, so it is not surprising that the innovation averages by responses to it show that those most positively oriented towards innovation should disagree with the idea that policy decisions are the exclusive right of the highest executive in the organization. That the responses have such a direct and strong relation to the innovation scores, however, throws a little light upon the innovation scores themselves. It will be remembered that the items least subscribed to by the respondents were those which had to do with changing or breaking established rules and regulations. Higher scores indicate an increased willingness to break or change regulations and to trust subordinates to control themselves, both important values if a policy of decision-making decentralization is to succeed.

TABLE 46. Decentralization of Decision-making Power: Efficiency and Innovation Averages by Response Category

		%	Efficiency Average	Innovation Average
Decisions on new policies	completely disagree	14	45	25
should be made exclusively	disagree	32	31	16
by the highest	agree	34	35	14
hierarchical level.	completely agree	20	39	3
	NR = 1			

Efficiency, on the other hand, does not seem to be a central factor in attitudes towards the delegation of authority. While those completely against a concentration of authority in the highest hierarchical levels are also those most concerned with efficiency, those completely in favor of such an arrangement are also above average in their concern with efficiency. The least emphatic responses to this item are given by respondents who seem to be less concerned with efficiency than those completely for or against the idea. A possible conclusion is that efficiency criteria lead to a rejection of the item. In both cases, however, those most concerned with efficiency and innovation completely disagreed with the idea that decisions on new policies should be made exclusively by the highest hierarchical level.

A breakdown of responses by job level and type reveals that line department heads are most in favor of the decentralization of authority and line noncommand pereonnel most opposed. Department heads in general oppose the item (9 to 6) and line intermediate command respondents also oppose it (22 to 19). Staff analysts are evenly split on the issue, and line noncommand respondents feel pretty much the opposite of their department heads (78 percent in favor of centralization for noncommand respondents, 75 percent opposed for department chiefs). Staff command respondents as a whole favor centralized authority by 57 percent, while line command respondents reject it by 57 percent.

Two explanations suggest themselves. First, staff personnel in the Venezuelan system are ordinarily attached to executive offices at the upper levels of the hierarchy. Because of this they may feel that if decisions on policies are made at lower levels their input will not be used. This would explain why all levels of staff respondents were in favor of retaining the present system of centralized decision making. On the other hand, between 43 and 49 percent of all staff groups were opposed to the item. It is possible that these respondents recognized that if authority were delegated to lower command echelons, staff support would very likely also be decentralized, so that their input would continue at a lower and more immediate operational level.

The second explanation is that if command power is decentralized, the first to feel the effects of this policy will be the line department heads. Given this situation, it is not surprising that they are in favor of more authority for themselves. The same argument, with somewhat less force because of their increased distance from the highest hierarchical level mentioned in the item, may be made for the intermediate line chiefs. In this case their relative lack of enthusiasm could be explained by the lesser likelihood of their receiving the policy-making authority. Line noncommand respondents, however, are highly unlikely to receive any policy-making authority; a conclusion that can be drawn from the above analysis is that given this situation they would much prefer that their supervisors be denied this power also. Why this should be is not a question answerable from the data, but it may be that this response is simply part of the general commitment to the status quo that this group has consistently demonstrated throughout the study.

On the whole, staff respondents agree that basic decision making should be highly centralized, and are more in agreement as they rise in rank. Line respondents on command levels show the reverse pattern, disagreeing more as they attain higher command positions.

The "Islands of Reform" Strategy of Administrative Reform

One major implication of our discussion of the history of the Public Administration Commission was that given the strength of the present bureaucratic organizations, the best policy for the commission is to concentrate its efforts upon the relatively few organizations positively oriented towards administrative reform, i.e., those that are ready to cooperate with the commission. Although the legislation recommended by the commission continues to be cast in comprehensive terms, its implementation through the ORCA offices is essentially through these "islands of reform." As a general theory, however, our respondents reject the idea of selective reform by an overwhelming majority (Table 47). They very obviously feel that the entire public administration is in need of reform and that the commission should not exclude any organization from its endeavors.

On the other hand, if the question is more sharply focused upon the implementation of policy, a quite different pattern of responses results (Table 48). Forty-five percent of the respondents agree that selective reform efforts are desirable when emphasis is placed upon the implementation of development policies. Line respondents are less in favor of the item than staff, 60 percent of them opposing the item as opposed to 51 percent of the staff respondents. This may be because line respondents do not feel that they should be singled out for reforms over other groups, since they are the respondents most closely associated with the actual implementation of development policies.

TABLE 47. Response to Items on Selective and Comprehensive
Administrative Reform

		%
In order to give good results, administrative reform should concentrate on only a few organizations.	completely disagree	43
	disagree	53
	agree	3
	completely agree	1
	NR = 1	
In order to give good results, administrative administrative reform should cover the entire public administration.	completely agree	64
	agree	29
	disagree	7
	completely disagree	0
	NR = 0	

TABLE 48. Selective Reform of Policy-implementing Agencies:
Efficiency and Innovation Averages by Response Category

		%	Efficiency Average	Innovation Average
For administrative reform to give good results, it should concentrate on those organizations most directly related to the implementation of specific development policies.	completely disagree	15	38	28
	disagree	40	35	10
	agree	39	34	13
	completely agree	6	46	15
	NR = 1			

The only group by job level and type that does agree with the item is staff intermediate chiefs. These respondents favor this kind of selective reform by 66 percent, the next closest group being line noncommand respondents, of whom 44 percent agree. From the data available there is no particular explanation for this agreement, since the staff intermediate command respondents proved to be about average on both the efficiency and innovation scales and since there is no theoretical reason why they should favor this type of reform more than the other groups.

A division by innovation and efficiency scales indicates that on an agree/disagree basis the respondents are much the same. Those who agree with the item average 13 on the innovation scale and 35 on the effciency scale, while those on the opposite side average 15 and 36. Those who completely disagree with the item are substantially above the average (28) on the innovation scale, while the same is true of those who completely agree on the efficiency scale (46). From this it could be argued that those most concerned with innovation do not see the strategy envisioned by the item as innovative, while those most concerned with efficiency do see it as a positive means of achieving that value. Given the close average scores of all those who agreed or disagreed, however, this is a fairly tenuous assumption. The safest conclusion to be drawn from the data is probably that the respondents are by and large opposed to the item by a thin margin.

The converse of this, of course, is that a substantial number of respondents view development agencies as the most important focus of administrative reform and agree that those organizations engaged in it should be given precedence over those that are not. Since these same respondents earlier agreed that all of the public administration should be the subject of reform, this would seem to be an important qualification.

On the specific question of the application of the "islands of reform" strategy, an approach that the respondents overwhelmingly rejected, opinion is also divided. Whereas the previous item focused upon development agencies, these final items concentrate upon the quality of the organizations involved (Table 49).

It is evident that the respondents are generally agreed that agencies should not be singled out for reform solely because they desire to be reformed. On the other hand, those who agreed with this item averaged 41 on the efficiency index, while those who disagreed averaged 34. The obvious conclusion is that those most concerned with efficiency saw the strategy as an efficient one. The corresponding innovation scores were 6 and 16, so apparently those most concerned with innovation did not see this as an innovative approach. In both cases, those holding strong opinions were most likely to be positively oriented towards innovation and efficiency than those who had moderate opinions.

The only group by job level and type that was significantly different from the general response was that of line department heads, 43 percent of whom agreed with the strategy of concentrating upon those agencies desiring to be reformed. The other groups all fell

TABLE 49. Strategies in the "Islands of Reform" Approach to Reform
(Quality of Organizations): Efficiency and Innovation
Averages by Response Category

		%	Efficiency Average	Innovation Average
If administrative reform efforts are concentrated on only some agencies, these agencies should be those which desire to be re-formed, even though they may be fairly efficient already.	completely disagree	11	41	25
	disagree	65	33	15
	agree	21	40	4
	completely agree	3	48	19
	NR = 3			
If administrative reform efforts are concentrated on only some agencies, these agencies should be those which are most in need of reform.	completely disagree	5	35	26
	disagree	36	30	11
	agree	43	38	12
	completely agree	16	45	18
	NR = 3			

within 10 points of the general response. Since the line department heads averaged the highest innovation and efficiency scores of any group, it would perhaps be reasonable to argue that this result is especially significant. That is, line department heads have a high degree of experience with the implementation of policy and are also strongly motivated towards both innovation and efficiency; therefore their opinion upon the implementation of administrative reform should carry special weight. Even if this argument is accepted, however, the line department heads are still 57 percent in disagreement with the item. This may be substantially less than the other groups, but it is still less than a majority for this particular strategy of reform.

The contrary strategy, that of concentrating upon those agencies most in need of reform (Table 49, item 2), was more controversial. The respondents' attitudes towards innovation do not seem especially important, although those with extreme responses again tended to be those in favor of innovation. All those who agreed with the item averaged 14, while those who disagreed averaged 13.

On the other hand, the very few respondents who totally disagreed with the item had the highest innovation score (26).

There is quite strong evidence that those most concerned with efficiency tended to agree with the item. Those in agreement averaged 40, while those opposed averaged 30. This, coupled with a like response to item 1, argues that those of our respondents who are especially efficiency-minded prefer either of the two strategies to one which does not differentiate among the agencies to be reformed. That is, given that all government agencies are in need of reform, the reform agency should still concentrate upon some rather than all.

It is interesting to note that staff division or section chiefs are most in favor of the approach that concentrates upon those agencies most in need of reform. This is the only group in favor of concentrating reform efforts upon those organizations most directly related to the implementation of specific development policies and is also the most in favor of concentrating upon those agencies most in need of reform. It is the only group that given the "islands of reform" approach, has identified a particular sort of agency as that which the reforming agency ought to concentrate upon. Unfortunately, the data give no real clues as to why they have responded in this manner.

In sum, there is some recognition among the respondents that an efficient approach to administrative reform dictates a concentration upon those agencies that are most directly concerned with the implementation of specific development policies and that also desire to be reformed. This is not considered a particularly innovative approach to reform, nor does it receive great support from any single group. It seems to be a rather reluctant admission by those most concerned with the problem. It is certainly not anything approaching a solid endorsement of this policy by the majority of the respondents. What does receive a practically unanimous endorsement is the idea that administrative reform should cover the entire public administration, concentrating equally upon all the agencies within it. Unfortunately, this approach has proved to be manifestly impossible for the Public Administration Commission to implement.

PART III

CONCLUSIONS

XI.

CHANGE AND BUREAUCRACY

Public administration in Venezuela has three broad problem areas: (1) the relations among organizations and with the office of the president; (2) the authority structures and relations within organizations; and (3) the accountability of the bureaucracy. All three can be profitably approached through an examination of the concepts of authority and control. This relation is central to an understanding of bureaucracy, and especially to bureaucracy in a changing society.

The basic argument is that as authority is concentrated in one or a few offices, effective control of the actual implementation of policy becomes more and more difficult. The usual response is to tighten regulations and fiscal accountability in an effort to regain control. Such an effort involves the restriction of discretion at the middle and lower levels of the administration and can best be seen as an effort to impose the classical Weberian model even more strictly upon the bureaucracy. The result, unfortunately, is an even greater concentration of authority and consequently a greater lack of real control.

This is largely caused by the multiple norms held by administrators. While they may believe in the legitimacy of regulations and Weberian norms, bureaucrats also believe in many other norms (e.g., family or party responsibilities) that may in particular cases contradict their bureaucratic values. When this occurs they will act according to the values that seem to them stronger in the particular case. The classic example of this behavior in Latin America is the "obedezco pero no cumplo" doctrine of the colonial years, an explicit recognition of the legitimacy of the king's authority and his simultaneous lack of actual control. The contradictory aspects of "I obey but will not comply" can only be understood in this light.

The lack of continuing control of organizations as such by the central executive is also understandable in the light of more orthodox administrative theory. The concept of span of control centers upon the inability of any single executive to control more than a relatively small number of direct subordinates. The reasoning is that as direct subordinates multiply and the executive's time remains finite, he becomes increasingly unable to assimilate the information needed to make correct decisions. In a crisis such a system is capable of generating intense energy.and highly successful implementation of specific goals in specific instances. It does so by concentrating the attention of national and organizational executives upon particular projects. The number of critical projects in a nation undergoing the rapid changes that Venezuela is experiencing, however, practically ensures that concentration of attention upon specific projects will occur only under crisis conditions. A crisis mentality may very well develop and crisis management become the order of the day.

Such a situation leads to delay and stagnation on the operational level. The retention of authority at the upper levels of the bureaucracy has as its purpose and consequence the absence of authority by which operational personnel can deal with situations not foreseen by regulations. On the other hand, the information necessary to adapt the regulations to the changed conditions creates a bottleneck when sent to the top because of the mass of specific detail it contains. Only a few top executives are engaged in making decisions on bureaucratic problems, and consequently they find themselves immersed in details important to specific cases but not to overall policy. The middle and lower level bureaucrats who are aware of this information because of the nature of their jobs are at the same time denied the authority to decide these smaller questions of policy as they arise.

In a society with a slower rate of societal and economic change than Venezuela's the problem would not be as acute, for the rules and regulations finally promulgated at the higher levels would not be as out of date as they are likely to be in a situation involving more rapid change, and the bottleneck of information at the top would not be as clogged, since less information would be traveling up. It is unlikely that the pace of development in Venezuela will slow in the near future, however, and consequently the bureaucratic situation will also remain unchanged.

Seen in a historical perspective the Venezuelan bureaucracy is attempting to cope with problems of a rapidly developing nation with methods and authority patterns that evolved over hundreds of years in administrations designed to create and maintain a stable and unchanging culture. Such a system served the Spanish Empire very well indeed, but it has not functioned in the interests of an independent Venezuela. This has been especially true since the 1930s, when the government of Venezuela specifically accepted the task of guiding and creating a new Venezuela. Each government since then has reaffirmed its acceptance of the state's role in development, but the acceptance of the role and the development of an administrative apparatus capable of implementing development programs efficiently have proved to be separate phenomena.

Because of its revenues from oil, Venezuela has been able to survive and to learn from costly mistakes in implementation that a poorer country could not have afforded. The structural reorganization recently accomplished at the upper bureaucratic levels will, if it can overcome organizational resistance, relieve much of the pressure on the office of the president and allow more rational allocations of programs to organizations, as well as increase the possibility of better coordination among governmental organizations. Crises should be perceived by executives with authority to do something about them sooner under this system, and the costs of these crises should go down. In short, this reorganization confronts the first of the problems noted above, that of relations among organizations and with the office of the president.

This broad reorganization will not, however, change the behavior within the organizations themselves, nor will it change the authority structures which reflect that behavior. Insofar as it does not, the general administration of public policy will remain inefficient, punctuated by crisis responses which, while efficacious, are in most cases equally inefficient. The basic problem is that a sincere desire for increased efficiency on the part of the bureaucrats is contrary to an almost equally deep desire to maintain the existing authority patterns.

These patterns are characterized by the delegation of responsibility (formal authority) without the actual authority needed to accomplish the specified goals. Both the tradition of personalism and a reluctance to rely upon others lead to a concentration of real authority in the executive head of the unit of government involved. The cumulative effect of this process is the concentration of authority in the organizational executive (and through him in the presidency) and the consequent loss of control already described.

The integration of authority and control recommended by our analysis requires a delegation of meaningful authority to the middle echelons of the public service in the expectation that span of control and information problems will be solvable at this level. If this is the case, control will pass upward to these officials and over-all policy authority will remain with top executives, since their own span of control problems will have been greatly alleviated through the authority delegated to their immediate subordinates. It is essential in this design that single-problem information stop at the middle level of bureaucracy. If it continues to the higher levels, information channels will remain clogged, crises will continue to be the usual state of affairs, and delays and inefficiency will continue to result.

A very encouraging finding of the present study is that department heads, and especially line department heads, are the respondents most consistently positive towards both efficiency and innovation. That department heads are positively oriented towards these values indicates that their resistance to an increased delegation of authority and more efficient patterns of decision making within organizations would be less than than of any other group in the study. It is also encouraging that neither innovation nor efficiency scores showed any particular relationship with age or type of organization. Reform need not wait upon the young nor upon a compete reorganization of institutions.

Though neither age nor experience seem to have any particular bearing upon a respondent's attitude towards efficiency, the same cannot be said of the attitudes shown towards innovation. While age remains irrelevant, the respondent's time in the public service seems to be quite important. The data show an increasing openness to innovation with increased experience until, somewhere between six and nine years in the public service, interest begins to fall off. The respondents then become less and less interested in challenging established authority patterns as their time in the public service increases. Promotion seems to postpone the decline, and there is some indication that department heads have a propensity to retain their favorable attitudes towards innovation at a very high level. The implication is that noncommand and intermediate command personnel will generally be most ready to learn about reform and the different methods of innovation between six to nine years into their careers.

The Public Administration and the government have already demonstrated their belief that a geographical dispersion of authority is needed if regional development is to succeed through the formal administrative regionalization of the country. It is heartening to note, in this context, that respondents working in the interior are above average in their concerns for efficiency and, when adjustments are made for the sexual composition of the two groups, slightly above average in their orientation towards innovation. Since a dispersal of authority will be highly innovative, this finding indicates that reformers should make special efforts to reach those administrators outside Caracas. Their attitudes towards the increased authority given the regional offices (if any is actually given) might well be the critical factor in the success or failure of regionalization.

In the area that this study has argued is the most crucial for administrative reform, that of the dispersal of decision-making power within organizations in an effort to integrate authority and control, the study results are mildly positive. Respondents strongly oriented towards efficiency and innovation rejected the centralization of authority. Line command respondents also disagreed with the idea that basic policy making should occur only at the highest levels of authority. Since these respondents are those who would implement the new policy, these are encouraging results. The fact that line noncommand respondents and all staff respondents agreed with the present system indicates the scope of the problem.

Necessity has dictated a selective approach to reform on the part of the commission. It is clear from the record that if it could the commission would concentrate upon comprehensive reforms rather than single organizations. In this it is joined by the respondents, for they overwhelmingly support the idea that administrative reform should reach the entire public administration. When forced to make specific choices between agencies to be reformed, however, they agreed that the commission is following the best policy available to it in concentrating upon those agencies that are positively oriented towards reform.

Our analysis of the backgrounds of the respondents and their attitudes towards family and personal responsibilities has given strong support to the emphasis prismatic theory places upon polynormativeness. The relationships between personal priority and innovation scores in particular indicate a strong inverse relation between the strength of extended family ties and the degree of innovation acceptable to the respondent. With another focus, however, high personal priority scores were associated with high efficiency scores. That efficiency and innovation scores were themselves positively associated indicates the degree to which intervening variables entered into our respondents' thoughts.

Prismatic theory holds that no single-norm explanation of phenomena such as administrative values is likely to be satisfactory. Our investigations have shown that many variables have had strong effects upon the attitudes our respondents hold towards efficiency, innovation, and contravention of administrative criteria. Perhaps the most important conclusion we can draw from our data is that administrative factors proved to be more important than personal factors in the attitudes held by our respondents. This means that adult socialization and learning, both factors that the Public Administration Commission and the agencies themselves can influence, are most important in shaping the attitudes of our respondents.

Job levels were consistently the most important of all our variables in analyzing innovation and efficiency scores. Job location also proved decisive in predicting efficiency concerns, while cultural change in childhood seemed to have very positive effects upon innovation scores. Combinations of these and other factors are needed if we are to understand the components of choice that are important to our respondents. In order to understand polynormative choice we must first understand the nature and strength of the norms involved.

Generally speaking, we have found support for Hagen's thesis that status deprivation results in positive attitudes towards innovation. Lerner's thesis that urbanization is a cause of "modernization" was not sustained by our data, although it is clear that respondents from completely nonurban backgrounds did tend to have low innovation scores. What did result in more "modern" attitudes was a childhood that combined different cultures. Even so, Andinos (even those raised partly in Caracas) had a very strong pattern of high efficiency and low innovation and a/p scores. This leads to the supposition that efficiency and rectitude in office are more easily combined with traditional family ties than the change in traditional authority relations envisioned in the innovation items.

It is clear that at least some Venezuelan governmental organizations are well run and efficiently meeting their overt goals. Excellence within the system is not impossible. On the other hand, Venezuela can ill afford a system of public administration in which only a few agencies are able effectively to deliver the substance of governmental policy. Given the nation's cultural and historical background, it is unlikely that thoroughgoing internal reforms will be accomplished any time soon, or that they would be extremely beneficial if they were. The record indicates that motivation for performance is crucial, and that accountability is the primary factor in motivation. Historically, Venezuelan governments have held bureaucrats more accountable for their latent functions than for overt goals. The results have been inefficiency in achieving overt goals and crisis leadership.

The major effect of the democratic regimes that began in 1958 has been to render the bureaucracy accountable to at least part of the masses for the implementation of the overt goals of the government. It can be argued that this has been a major motivating force even for the CVG, the agency most successful in separating itself from the "people problems" so crucial to the appeal of the political parties. The patron/client relationship that is the fundamental factor in Venezuelan mass politics functions to put pressure on the bureaucracy to deliver the goods of public policy. This pressure is biased, personal, and political, but it is more pressure for the fulfillment of overt goals than the Venezuelan bureaucracy as a whole has ever had before.

The bureaucratic changes envisioned by reformers may or may not become law, but it is my opinion that without the sort of pressure patron/client politics put on the bureaucracy they will not result in positive benefits for the Venezuelan people. Given the pressure of internal reformers and innovative goals, bureaucrats of good will may have the leverage they need to move the Venezuelan bureaucracy from its inheritance of colonial conservatism and republican weakness to a position in which it can implement the changes necessary if Venezuela is to fulfill her promise to her people.

NOTES

CHAPTER 1

1. Various writers have remarked upon this tendency. Talton F. Ray gives it extended treatment in his *Politics of the Barrios of Venezuela*. Mark W. Cannon, R. Scott Fosler, and Robert Witherspoon see it as one of the major problems in the coordination of agency work at the local level in *Urban Government for Valencia, Venezuela*. John Kirby's "Venezuela's Land Reform" sees the same mechanism at work in the land reform program.

2. See Franklin Tugwell, *The Politics of Oil in Venezuela*, for an excellent analysis of oil and Venezuelan oil policy.

3. While most of the supporting evidence for this statement comes from my own experience in the Venezuelan university system, more scientific investigations of this phenomen in Venezuela have been made: see Robert F. Arnove, *Student Alienation: A Venezuelan Study*, and Dieter K. Zschock, Aníbal Fernández, George W. Schuyler, and W. Ramond Duncan, "The Education-Work Transition of Venezuelan University Students." The latter article in particular points out the friendship and family networks that support the maintenance of the value system, concluding that both "modern" and "traditional" criteria coexist. The position I have taken is that both criteria do exist but that the "traditional" is more powerful within the school system itself.

4. See especially Cannon, Fosler, and Witherspoon, *Urban Government for Valencia*, pp. 22–24.

5. I draw mainly upon my experiences here, but it is noteworthy that Fred W. Riggs, *Administration in Developing Countries: The Theory of Prismatic Society*, p. 113, sees the same phenomena occuring in most transitional governments.

6. Ibid., p. 282.

CHAPTER 2

1. While the discussion at this point draws upon most of my background in Latin American history and culture, and particularly upon Herring and Hanke, many of the details and the structure of the argument are based upon Mark Hanson's article directly relating these variables to the Venezuelan Ministry of Education, "Organizational Bureaucracy in Latin America and the Legacy of Spanish Colonialism."

2. See Lewis Hanke, *The Spanish Struggle for Justice in the Conquest of America*.

3. Data for this section have been taken from Enrique A. Martinez, "Los Ministerios in Venezuela."

4. Fred W. Riggs, *Administration in Developing Countries: The Theory of Prismatic Society*; also his "Bureaucrats and Political Development."

5. Roderick T. Groves, "Administrative Reform in Venezuela, 1958–1963," p. 22.

6. In 1945 a military coup set the stage for the first legal election that involved mass-based parties. The Acción Democrática won and instituted many reforms but was overthrown by another military coup in 1948. The general consensus is that the Acción Democrática attempted too many fundamental changes at once while forgetting that the military were still the final arbiters of Venezuelan politics.

7. The basic source for this information comes from Oscar Gomez Navaz, "La Administración Autónoma."

CHAPTER 3

1. See John Duncan Powell, "Peasant Society and Clientelist Politics," as well as his more extended work on the subject, *Political Mobilization of the Venezuelan Peasant*.

2. John Kirby, "Venezuela's Land Reform."

3. This system of attainment has been theoretically developed by Fred W. Riggs in *Administration in Developing Countries: The Theory of Prismatic Society*, p. 167.

4. Mark Hanson, "Organizational Bureaucracy," pp. 208–14.

5. John R. Dinkelspiel has done extensive work on this subject, especially in his dissertation, "Administrative Style and Economic Development: The Organization and Management of the Guayana Region Development of Venezuela," and in "Technology and Tradition: Regional and Urban Development in the Guayana." The negative consequences of such a strategy are clearly indicated in Dinkelspiel's works and in Lisa Peattie's *The View from the Barrio*. A different approach to the same problem is found in Noel McGinn and Russell G. Davis, *Build a Mill, Build a City, Build a School*.

CHAPTER 4

1. The basic work on CORDIPLAN remains John Friedmann's *Venezuela: From Doctrine to Dialogue*. See also Fred D. Levy, Jr., "Economic Planning in Venezuela."

2. A basic document for FUNDACOMUN is the final report submitted to the Ford Foundation-Institute of Public Administration by the Institute of Public Administration, New York, "Technical Aid Program to Fundación para el Desarrollo de la Comunidad y Fomento Municipal (FUNDACOMUN), Venezuela, April 1, 1963, through December 31, 1968." Mark W. Cannon, R. Scott Fosler, and Robert Witherspoon, *Urban Government for Valencia, Venezuela* contains additional information on FUNDACOMUN.

3. Lisa Peattie, *The View from the Barrio*, throughout, but especially p. 135.

4. The best short analysis of the life and times of the Public Administration Commission is Organization of American States, Unidad Tecnica de Administración Pública, "Venezuela: Evaluación de la estrategia para la reforma administrativa del gobierno central." Roderick T. Groves has treated the same subject in a more extended fashion in "Administrative Reform in Venezuela, 1958–1963" and in "Administrative Reform and Politics of Reform: The Case of Venezuela" and "The Venezuelan Administrative Reform Movement, 1958–1963."

5. Edwin Lieuwin, *Venezuela*, p. 181.

6. See David J. Gould, *Report: The Venezuelan Public Administration Education System*.

CHAPTER 5

1. Richard W. Adams, *The Second Sowing: Power and Secondary Development in Latin America*, p. 20.

2. Ibid., p. 23.

3. David C. McClelland, *The Achieving Society*.

4. Everett Hagen, *On the Theory of Social Change*.

5. Daniel Lerner, *The Passing of Traditional Society*.

6. Fred W. Riggs, *Administration in Developing Countries: The Theory of Prismatic Society*, p. 36.

7. Fred W. Riggs, *Thailand*, p. 369.

8. Riggs, *Administration in Developing Countries*, pp. 280–83.

9. Morroe Berger, *Bureaucracy and Society in Modern Egypt*.

10. Robert T. Daland and Paulo Matta, "Performance in the Brazilian Bureaucracy" (in process). See also Daland's article "Attitudes Toward Change Among Brazilian Bureaucrats," which gives Brazilian responses to the questions on efficiency and innovation used in this study.

11. Jack W. Hopkins, *The Government Executive of Modern Peru*.

12. W. Lloyd Warner, et al., *The American Federal Executive*.

13. Jerry Weaver, "Value Patterns of a Latin American Bureaucracy," pp. 225–33.

BIBLIOGRAPHY

Adams, Richard N. *The Second Sowing: Power and Secondary Development in Latin America*. San Francisco: Chandler, 1967.

Arnove, Robert F. *Student Alienation: A Venezuelan Study*. New York: Praeger, 1971.

Berger, Morroe. *Bureaucracy and Society in Modern Egypt*. Princeton: Princeton University Press, 1957.

Blank, David Eugene. *Politics in Venezuela*. Boston: Little, Brown, 1973.

Bonilla, Frank. *The Failure of Elites*. The Politics of Change in Venezuela, vol. 2. Cambridge: MIT Press, 1970.

Bonilla, Frank; and Silva Michelena, José A.; eds. *A Strategy for Research on Social Policy*. The Politics of Change in Venezuela, vol. 1. Cambridge: MIT Press, 1967.

Brewer-Carias, Allan-Randolph. *El proceso de reforma administrativa en Venezuela*. Caracas: Oficina de Información, Serie Conceptos, 1970.

Cannon, Mark W.; Fosler, R. Scott; and Witherspoon, Robert. *Urban Government for Valencia, Venezuela*. New York: Praeger, 1973.

Daland, Robert T. "Attitudes Toward Change Among Brazilian Bureaucrats," *Journal of Comparative Administration* 4, no. 2 (1972): 167–205.

――――. *Brazilian Planning: Development Politics and Administration*. Chapel Hill: The University of North Carolina Press, 1967.

――――, and Motta, Paulo. *Performance in the Brazilian Bureaucracy*. In process.

Dinkelspiel, John R. "Administrative Style and Economic Development: The Organization and Management of the Guayana Region Development of Venezuela." Ph.D. dissertation, Harvard University, 1967.

――――. "Technology and Tradition: Regional and Urban Development in the Guayana." Unpublished, no date.

Friedmann, John. *Regional Development Policy: A Case Study of Venezuela*. Cambridge: MIT Press, 1966.

――――. *Venezuela: From Doctrine to Dialogue*. Syracuse, N.Y.: Syracuse University Press, 1965.

Gomez, Rudolph. *The Peruvian Administrative System*. Boulder: University of Colorado Press, 1969.

Gómez Navas, Oscar, ed. "Administración Venezolana." Caracas: Programa Conjunta de Adiestramiento Pública, Comisión de Administración Pública, 1961.

———. "Los Institutos Autónomos." In "Administración Venezolana," edited by Oscar Gómez Navas. Caracas: Programa Conjunta de Adiestramiento, Comisión de Administración Pública, 1961.

———. *Manual para el Estudio del Regimen Constitucional y Administrativo de Venezuela*. Caracas: Comisión de Administración Pública, 1967.

Gould, David J. *Report: The Venezuelan Public Administration Education System*. Caracas: Escuela Normal de Administración Pública, 1962.

Graham, Lawrence A. *Civil Service Reform in Brazil: Principles versus Practice*. Austin: University of Texas Press, 1968.

Groves, Roderick T. "Administrative Reform and the Politics of Reform: The Case of Venezuela." *Public Administration Review* 27 (December 1967): 436–45.

———. "Administrative Reform in Venezuela, 1958–1963." Ph.D. dissertation, University of Wisconsin, 1965.

———. "The Venezuelan Administrative Reform Movement, 1958–1963." In *Development Administration in Latin America*, edited by Clarence E. Thurber and Lawrence S. Graham. Durham: Duke University Press, 1973.

Hagen, Everett. *On the Theory of Social Change*. Homewood, Ill.: Dorsey Press, 1962.

Hanke, Lewis. *The Spanish Struggle for Justice in the Conquest of America*. Boston: Little, Brown, 1965.

Hanson, Mark. "Organizational Bureaucracy in Latin America and the Legacy of Spanish Colonialism." *Journal of Interamerican Studies and World Affairs* 16, no. 2 (May 1974): 199–200.

Herring, Hubert. *A History of Latin America*. 2d ed. New York: Alfred A. Knopf, 1965.

Hopkins, Jack W. *The Government Executive of Modern Peru*. Gainesville: University of Florida Press, 1967.

Institute of Public Administration, New York. "Technical Program to Fundación para el Desarollo de la Comunidad y Fomento Municipal (FUNDACOMUN), Venezuela, April 1, 1963, through December 31, 1968." [Final report submitted to the Ford Foundation and the Institute of Public Administration]. New York:

Karst, Kenneth L.; Schwartz, Murray L.; and Schwartz, Audrey J. *The Evolution of Law in the Barrios of Caracas*. Latin American Studies, vol. 20. Los Angeles: Latin American Center, University of California, 1973.

Kirby, John. "Venezuela's Land Reform." *Journal of Interamerican Studies and World Affairs* 15, no. 2 (May 1973): 205–20.

LaBelle, Thomas J. *The New Professional in Venezuelan Secondary Education*. Latin American Studies, vol. 23. Los Angeles: Latin American Center, University of California, 1973.

Lerner, Daniel. *The Passing of Traditional Society*. New York: The Free Press, 1958.

Levine, Daniel H. *Conflict and Political Change in Venezuela*. Princeton: Princeton University Press, 1973.

Levy, Fred D., Jr. "Economic Planning in Venezuela." In *Development Administration in Latin America*, edited by Clarence E. Thurber and Lawrence S. Graham. Durham: Duke University Press, 1973.

Lieuwin, Edwin. *Venezuela*. London and New York: Oxford University Press, 1961.

Marrero y Artiles, Leví. *Venezuela y sus recursos*. Caracas: Cultural Venezolana, 1964.

Martínez, Enrique A. "Los Ministerios en Venezuela." In "Administración Venezolana," edited by Oscar Gómez Navaz. Mimeographed. Caracas: Programa Conjunta de Adiestramiento Pública, Comisión de Administración Pública, 1961.

McClelland, David C. *The Achieving Society*. New York: The Free Press, 1961.

McGinn, Noel F.; and Davis, Russell G. *Build a Mill, Build a City, Build a School*. Cambridge: MIT Press, 1969.

Organization of American States. Unidad Técnica de Administración Pública. "Venezuela: Evaluación de la estrategia para la reforma admistrativa del gobierno central." Washington, D.C.: Departamento de Asuntos Economicos Organización de Los Estados Americanos, 1970.

Peattie, Lisa. *The View from the Barrio*. Ann Arbor: University of Michigan Press, 1968.

Powell, John Duncan. "Peasant Society and Clientelist Politics." In *Political Development and Social Change*, edited by Jason L. Finkle and Richard W. Gable. 2nd edition. New York: John Wiley and Sons, 1971.

———. *Political Mobilization of the Venezuelan Peasant*. Cambridge: Harvard University Press, 1971.

Ray, Talton F. *The Politics of the Barrios of Venezuela*. Berkeley: University of California Press, 1969.

Riggs, Fred W. *Administration in Developing Countries: The Theory of Prismatic Society*. Boston: Houghton Mifflin, 1964.

———. "Bureaucrats and Political Development." In *Political Development and Social Change*, edited by Jason L. Finkle and Richard

W. Gable. 2nd edition. New York: John Wiley and Sons, 1971.
———. *Thailand*. Honolulu: East-West Center Press, 1966.
Siegel, Gilbert B. "The Strategy of Public Administration Reform: The Case of Brazil." *Public Administration Review* 26 (March 1966):45–55.
Silva Michelena, José Agustin. *The Illusion of Democracy in Dependent Nations*. The Politics of Change in Venezuela, vol. 3. Cambridge: MIT Press, 1971.
Tugwell, Franklin. *The Politics of Oil in Venezuela*. Stanford: Stanford University Press, 1975.
Venezuela. Comisíon de Administración Pública [CAP]. *Lineamientos generales de la reforma administrativa*. Caracas, 1970.
———. Comisión de Administración Pública. *La reforma administrativa en Venezuela (1969–1971)*. Caracas: Comisión de Administracíon Pública, 1971.
———.Comisión de Administración Pública. *La reforma de toda la administración pública por toda la administración pública*. Caracas: 1970.
———. Oficina Central de Información.
———. Universidad Central, Caracas. Centro de Estudios del Desarollo. *Muestras de Empleados Publicos*. Estudio de conflictos y consenso: Serie de resultados parciales, no. 7. Caracas: CENDES, 1967.
Warner, William Lloyd, et al. *The American Federal Executive*. New Haven: Yale University Press, 1964.
Weaver, Jerry. "Value Patterns of a Latin American Bureaucracy." *Human Relations* 23 (June 1970):225–33.
Zschock, Dieter K.; Fernández, Aníbal; Schuyler, George W.; and Duncan, W. Raymond. "The Education–Work Transition of Venezuelan University Students." *Journal of Interamerican Studies and World Affairs* 16, no. 1 (February 1974):96–118.

INDEX